Living The Nightmare
Becoming The Dream

Published 2017 by Temple DPS.

British Library Cataloguing in Publication Data
A catalogue record for this book is available from the British Library.

ISBN: 978-0-9562432-6-3

Design and print management: G & J Hughes

Living The Nightmare
Becoming The Dream

A bodybuilder's tale

John McLoughlin

Introduction

When I was about five or six, my teacher asked what I wanted to do for a job when I got older. I said I wanted to be a bodybuilder. The teacher said being a bodybuilder wasn't a real job!
"Well," I said, "that's what I'm going to be!"

I was looking through a bodybuilding magazine, around five or six years of age. I remember seeing a guy, his name Samir Bannout. He was with a girl, she had blonde hair, blue eyes and was slim in stature, both of them happily smiling, enjoying the twilight skies, the backdrop for this picture being Venice Beach, California, USA. It was dusky, possibly sunset, the skies beautiful, in various shades of red and orange. The guy donned a kite-like shape with large vascular arms and shoulders. He had chiselled, square features, carrying a smile that for me would represent confidence. He looked to have it made.

I can't be sure whether it was just the guy's physique, or the confidence he so valiantly displayed, maybe it was the general setting in which the picture was taken, or perhaps it was the whole combination. The guy, the girl, the skies, the feeling I got when viewing the picture. Whichever it may have been, this had become my one true pursuit of happiness. The Dream.

Even before starting in bodybuilding, before having been influenced, even knowing what self-belief meant, I always had the desire to succeed in the things I most wanted to do. It was Christmas Day, 1977, I was three years of age at the time. I'd been busy opening presents then playing with my new cardboard Death Star and Star Wars figures when I heard my dad say, "John, you've not finished looking at the rest of your presents yet." He took my hand then walked me over to the other side of the room where a brand new bike was waiting for me. "Yes!", I thought. But it all went wrong when I noticed that the bike had been fitted with stabilisers. I started kicking off, saying I wanted them taken off, I wasn't happy with the bike at all now. I wouldn't even look at it until the stabilisers were gone. My mum said no, and I think I may have got a bit of a telling off too. It got to 1978 Easter spring break, I still hadn't touched or bothered with the bike. My dad suggested that I might try it out now that the weather had turned nice, but I was still adamant about the stabilisers. Eventually my dad agreed to dismantle them.

We were at the side of our white cottage, the street that we lived on having a moderate slope. On the right there was a road, and on the left a long hedge. I would have to use bricks to be able to climb on the bike as I wasn't tall enough at the time. It was time to ride the bike! I set off, assuming that once I got started, that was that, but I soon realised this wasn't the case as I slammed into the hedge, falling backwards off the bike. Quickly, I brushed myself off, ready to try again. This time I got that little bit further before falling off once more, now with the hedge cutting the side of my face, with my hands also cut due to the fall. My dad telling me I was being stupid as I climbed back on for a third attempt, my mum now coming out to see what's going on. I tried again now heading in the opposite direction, trying to avoid the hedge, but this time I went over on to the road then over the handle bars. I could hear my mum shouting "Mick, get him off that bloody bike before he kills his self." I got up crying, cuts and bruises everywhere, snotty faced and teary, frustrated by the failure.

At the start of the following week, the first day of the holidays, I had a plan. Still wanting to ride the bike, I would slip the bike through the fence before climbing over the fence escaping into the street. I then walked my bike down to the church grounds near to where the social club was, as I knew it had a step for me to climb on the bike. My daily assault started here. I was constantly trying, getting closer as I went. Come mid-week, my mum knew where I was and I remember her calling me in for tea from the top of the street most days. By Thursday I was getting close but still hadn't quite grasped it. On Friday my mum asked me not to go far as there were plans to go out, but I couldn't resist, I was out, not able to stay in as told. I'd been practicing around an hour, then all of a sudden I found the right balance, able to stay on the bike, really excited! When Mum and Dad drove down looking for me, I could see they were pretty mad, but I was standing there grinning, literally shaking with excitement about showing them what I had achieved. "Come on, quick", they said, but I was on the step, then I was on the bike then riding around in a wobbly little circle. I was over the moon, my mum and dad couldn't help but laugh, it was brilliant. This, my first achievement, determination, my initial gift from God.

Looking back, perhaps this was God's way (life's way) of showing me that in order to succeed in life, I must start by trying. There would be falls along the way, and other people may slow down the progress, so perhaps having to go out of the way, to go it alone may be the only answer. There will be blood, sweat and tears, frustration, but also when achieving a goal, something you had worked hard at yourself, there was a massive feel of excitement, life's natural high when achieving what you had set out to do. With how the rest of my life played out this could have easily been that message, but for me I'd like to keep it much simpler. If you like something, go for it, and like a child there's no analysing, no underlining message, just a straight up message of see it, do it, learn as you go, the childlike option being something I'd always go with, the adult side of things being how you stick with it when the initial excitement gets harder to keep with (injuries, age, life). It worked when riding the bike and again with all the other hobbies, sports I would be good at, even down to writing this book. If you work at anything hard enough, for long enough, and believe enough, the likelihood is, you will do OK, even if it's just improving by your own standards. Something to think about!

Where it all first started

I remember being in school aged five or six, the teacher asking everyone what they wanted to do for a job when they got older. Everyone said the usual things, like bus driver or policeman, but when my turn came I stood up and said I wanted to be a bodybuilder. The teacher replied that being a bodybuilder wasn't a real job! I remember feeling slightly offended. "Well," I said, "that's what I'm going to be!"

People·get into bodybuilding for numerous reasons. Some people do it to further an existing sport, then get a love for it. Some people do it as they may have been bullied, to no longer be seen as a target. There will be some who do it to be seen by the opposite sex, then there's those who will do it just to be seen. I wanted to do bodybuilding because I liked the look of it from the start.

My story starts way back when I used to be a big fan of The Incredible Hulk, the TV series from the 70s; I actually believed he was real, but this soon changed when I went to stay at my friend Sean's house. Sean's brothers were bodybuilding fans and showed me pictures in a magazine of Lou Ferrigno, the man who played the Hulk. I was in disbelief when looking at all the pictures, and instantly my curiosity grew as I looked at all the other bodybuilders in the mag.

Every time I went up to Sean's I asked to look at the magazines and, because of my interest, Sean's older brother Mike would tell me about certain bodybuilders. Mike showed me pictures of Tom Platz, an up-and-comer who had the biggest legs in the world. He told me Arnold Schwarzenegger was the best bodybuilder in the world, and that he was tipped to star in a new movie named Conan the Barbarian. He even showed me the book that Conan was based on, as he was a big fan. Within a couple of months, Mike had given me his entire stash of bodybuilding magazines, to keep, as I had rooted through them that often. In fact, every time I went to his house, I was sat looking through the magazines as the rest of the Joyce family were sat talking.

I remember my dad calling me into the front room as there was a documentary on TV showing bodybuilders being viewed as art. I couldn't get the images out of my head; I had become totally caught up with it all. My dad said I was too young to start training, and even when I reached my teens I should still only be lifting light until I was about 16 or 17, as he said that otherwise it could affect my bone development and growth. I'm not sure where he got this advice, but looking back now it wouldn't be far wrong. I knew I had to listen because the thought of limiting my potential in any way wasn't an option for me. When the time was right, I wanted to be fully functional and without any unnecessary limitations that could prevent me from being the best I could be. The initial dedication being to stay clear of the thing I most wanted to do. It was just a waiting game now.

I found other things to do, and became renowned for being a very good break dancer. I could say it was my first great passion but, although I had the best of times and competed at a high level, I never saw it for more than what it was; just a way to have a really good time. My sights were always firmly set on being a bodybuilder.

I was around thirteen years old when I lifted my first weight. My mate Des Hutchie had some weights and a weight bench rigged up in his back garden. I remember being really excited lifting the weights for the first time. Des was laughing; I don't think he could believe that someone could be so happy throwing a few sand-filled plastic weights around. I had started boxing by this time and had done quite well, winning a good few inter-club bouts. I had also got myself a paper-round and had told Graham, the guy who owned the shop, that I was into running and wanted the longest round he had. He gave me a round which I think must have been around five miles long, I then thanked him for it, as it would get me fit, helping me become a better runner for the school team. Years on Graham would tell everyone who knew me how he didn't think I was the full shilling. Because of the hills and the early starts, no one had ever wanted that round and no one had ever wanted it since. I kept with it until after leaving school.

Sylvester Stallone was the man I was most influenced by, the way his physique grew from movie to movie, I found astounding. So every morning, like Rocky in the movies I used to force myself to swallow two raw eggs in a glass before going out for my paper-round. Every single morning I would gag on those eggs, sometimes throwing up. I used to hold my hand over my mouth to make sure they went down, but I'd still feel ill because of the slimy taste. I followed this ritual from the age of thirteen until I was seventeen. Only then did I find out that you could boil or scramble the eggs, as it really didn't make a difference. I was a schoolboy and this was a schoolboy error indeed, but in my defence my only guidance on what to eat at this point was what I had seen in the Rocky movies. In fact most of my training and motivations at the time was based on what I had seen at the movies.

At Christmas I got my first set of weights. I got exactly the same set as Des, as he seemed to be getting big and I thought it had something to do with the type of weights he was using. I was extremely naïve to say the least. Come summer 1988 my dad had built a shed and said I could use it for my weights, as they were taking up too much room in the house. I thought it was just going to be an empty shed but he had kitted it out with wall bars, a chinning bar, and even hung my punch-bag up with all the weights, and the weight-bench at the back. He had put up a shelf for my stereo and even built in a few plug sockets so I could listen to music while training. I was over the moon. To begin with my dad hadn't been sure about me training, but when he did this for me, he took away any reason for me not to train, and I was going to make the most of it.

I put together what was my first real workout. It started with moderate weights but was high in repetitions and good form; but the majority of my workout would be aimed at body strength. I set my goals, which was as many sets as it took to get to 100 repetitions. I would follow this with chin-ups, press-ups and sit-ups, followed by bag-work. If I was training with my friend Dennis we would also go a round or two in the garden, usually ending up black and blue as I only had one pair of boxing gloves, so one glove each!

Before long my fitness had nearly tripled, I could do 50 to 60 chin-ups straight off, and could do 100 press-ups in one go. I had to extend my 'rep' range for sit-ups to between 300 and 350, as I could now do 150 sit-ups in one go.

SYLVESTER STALLONE WAS THE MAN I WAS MOST INFLUENCED BY

a series of wild parties
made me very popular
around school...

CHAPTER 1

Growing confidence in my school years

By this time I wasn't getting into as much trouble at school as I had been doing for the last couple of years. I had also stopped training at the boxing club as I now got more enjoyment training at home. I had more time with my friends as well. I developed an interest in skate-boarding and also played a bit of tennis. I had a good set of friends from both sides of the tracks, which escalated after throwing a series of wild parties that made me very popular around school.

I had a party-piece where I would ask someone, usually a girl, for a 10p-piece, then I would lift my shirt, flex my abs and stick the coin in, my abs would grab the coin keeping it upright. All the kids in class would find this really funny, so would tell their friends, so I would have to show them as well. Some would look amazed while others could only giggle.

I had several short-term girlfriends, but nothing very serious as think I enjoyed falling in love from week to week, and I had so many good cheesy chat-up lines that it would have been a shame to waste them. I wasn't really into homework (or any work when it came to school), and I'd copy most of my work from pals Simon and Porky, usually around ten minutes before going to class. I remember once copying Simon's course work for a geography project we had to do.

Simon said bluntly "Don't copy it word for word"... but I didn't know what 'word for word' meant, so I just copied it as it was written. The following week the teacher handed out the results. As I went to get mine, the teacher was smiling, "John, your work looks very much like Simon's". Simon got an A, I got an F, I just laughed, I wasn't bothered as long as I didn't have to stay behind and have to do detention. I was well liked by most teachers and tended to get away with a lot as I was cheeky yet funny with the only lessons I liked being sports, religion and drama. I never considered myself an under-achiever, as I was achieving in the things I wanted to do, it's just that my way was a little different to what the school board might want. I wasn't out to rebel, I was just out to be happy, to make others happy, to have fun essential for any kid. Life without logic.

I would say I was the school's cool kid at that time, I was the one the girls fancied and who the guys liked to hang out with. When things were going well I never looked for trouble, if anything I would only bully the kids that bullied others, so even the clever kids liked me. School life was fierce even if not quite for the right reasons.

I was in the fourth year at secondary school at this time, aged around fourteen or fifteen. I was captain of the running teams and was part of the rugby team. I was sponsored for skate-boarding and also worked as a Skate Warden at both the Leisure Centre and the Sports Centre and had skated amongst some of the best skaters in the world, including Steve Caballero and Tony Hawke. Even at this early stage I took any chance I got to take my shirt off, whether I was running around in games or skating around the city centre. I thought how great it would be when I got bigger; but looking back now, even though I was only eight stone or so, this would be the most carefree and confident about myself I would ever be.

I was influenced at this point by my older cousins, Nick Harrison and Phil Rose; they were my real-life childhood heroes. They were always shaped-up and looked well, and they used to get all the nice-looking girls, but I mainly liked them because they treated me well and didn't mind me tagging along with them even when I was quite young. I couldn't have asked for two better role-models whilst growing up. The other main influences in my life were film stars such as Arnold, Sly Stallone, Tom Cruise, Rob Lowe, Patrick Swayze, Kurt Russell and Jean-Claude Van Damme. Their movies always featured characters who had to rise up and overcome challenges greater than themselves, and most of them had some kind of moral spin-off that left you feeling motivated. This brings me to my next topic, which is what I consider to be my first motivational story.

I THOUGHT HOW GREAT IT WOULD BE WHEN I GOT BIGGER; BUT LOOKING BACK NOW, THIS WOULD BE THE MOST CAREFREE AND CONFIDENT ABOUT MYSELF I WOULD EVER BE.

Chapter 2

My first motivational story

It was early summer 1989, and every year all the kids at our school (St Gabriel's RC High School, Bury) did something to make money for a Christian charity named St Joseph's Penny. On this occasion I had decided I would see if I could do 50 chin-ups in a minute. I trained hard to do this and with people wanting to watch the event I obviously didn't want to mess up – and I never thought I would.

The day arrived, with the teacher (Mr Keating) opening up the sports hall. It was dinner-time so loads of kids had turned up to watch, and when the kids outside saw something was going on they all came to the side of the hall, peering in through the windows. I was buzzing at the turn-out, ready to strut my stuff. I stood under the chinning-bar while the teacher sat at the side, setting his stop-watch before looking at me to ask if I was ready. I nodded, then jumped up to grab the bar as he started his clock.

I was flying for the first 40 or so reps, then I felt my hands begin to slip, then my grip weaken. I kicked my legs and managed to drag myself up for another five or six reps, before my grip give out completely, with me dropping from the bar. I was massively frustrated, even though everyone in the sports hall was clapping, saying they would pay me anyway. Now angered, I climbed up on the bar to try again. I fell on my 40th rep this time, but didn't slip, I just didn't have the energy to do any more. I tried for a third time, but by now I could only get to nine reps. No one was clapping now, they were just looking at me, realizing how put-out and embarrassed about the whole event I had become.

I dropped my head, not able to make eye contact with anyone, but a voice in my head was saying "I need to do this". I knew I couldn't carry on straight away as I was exhausted, so I asked the teacher if I could come back the next day. He could see I was a little cut up about it, so just said "Yes, John, not a problem." When I got home I trained for as long as I could, doing as many 'chins' as possible. That night I watched the movies Youngblood staring Rob Lowe and Patrick Swayze, then No Retreat, No Surrender starring Jean-Claude Van Damme. These I watched for motivation. If you've not seen them, these films show the main star having a bad time then coming back to claim victory. I was now ready for the next day.

Dinner-time came again and as I entered the sports hall there was already a massive crowd inside, with the outside also rammed with kids end-to-end peering through the windows, shouting "Come on, John-boy". Once again, motivated and buzzing I stepped up to the bar, I glanced at the teacher who soon gave me the nod, I then set off with the same speed and determination as I had the day earlier.

Everyone was cheering, spurring me on, yet once again towards the end my grip was slipping... but this time I kept hold, throwing myself over the bar, thrusting on for dear life until finally I heard the teacher shout "50!" I jumped from the bar semi-hysterical, pounding the floor, running round flexing victoriously. The teacher smiled and gave me the thumbs-up, all the kids in the hall shouted and cheered, sharing my moment.

It wasn't the Olympics, or anything really to shout about, but for me it was the first event in which I had overcome failure and not given up on myself. I had learnt that sometimes it's not the event, but the determination of the individual doing the event that gets people motivated, and in this instance that was the case. Years down the line I would be approached by people who were there on that day, they would tell me how exciting it all was, and how everyone wanted to start training after watching it. But even better than this was the fact that the teacher who had given me his time as well as doing the time-keeping would use this in morning assembly, and would tell the story in reference to not giving up, and trying again if you fail. I found this very flattering, it was how I had wanted it to be seen. My sister, who is twelve years my junior, told me that the teacher was still telling the story even when she was at the school. Happy days.

Before I knew it I was
getting full of drink and
tablets, and all kinds of
pills and potions.

Chapter 3

Moving in the wrong direction

My final school year had arrived, and slowly but surely things were starting to change. No longer were abs and quiffy Tom Cruise haircuts all the rage; the girls were now chasing thin pale faces, long curtain-type haircuts, college lads with cars, and indie music fans. The brat-pack movies and lifestyle were quickly becoming forgotten, with most of my friends jumping on the band-wagon, talking like they were spaced-out or high. I thought it all pretty stupid, just hoping it was a phase they were going through.

At home things weren't so great. I had always had a great home life, and even when I had thrown a string of crazy parties with the house getting smashed to bits my parents had always been pretty cool about it somehow, so I'm not sure if I had finally burnt my bridges or whether they just had stuff on their minds but they seemed off, unapproachable around this time. I got into a fight at school and there was a good chance that I'd be expelled, but thankfully because of the circumstances surrounding the fight, and the fact it was nearly the end of term, I was able to stay on and sit my exams.

Initially leaving school was a blast. At the leavers' do, we turned up in a Rolls Royce all donning white suits, classic 80s prom style. We brought the house down. I'd been involved in acting throughout school, even getting involved doing a play with actress Gillian Kearney who had starred in the TV series Brookside, as well as starring earlier with actress Lisa Riley (Emmerdale) and movie screenwriter Neal Jaworski (Decoy Bride). This led to a couple of appearances as an extra on TV. I'd managed to do some modelling for a catalogue and had also been picked up to do the British Isles Pro-Skateboard Tour which would span five or six weeks, covering most of the holidays.

By the time I was back from the tour, things had moved on, with all my pals now massively into the club scene and generally getting trashed. I was keen to get started at the gym, but no one was interested in going, and even my shed was now being used to store tools as I'd been caught up in skateboarding so wasn't using it as often. I felt a bit down – no one was into skating any more, and the skateboard places where I had worked were now quiet, one of them had closed. No one wanted to train, but by the same note, I didn't want to leave the friends I'd been around for so long.

Being young and daft I jumped on the band wagon and decided to hit the party scene for now, hoping that by the time we started college I could be persuasive enough to get everyone down to the gym. It's funny when you're young, you think that you're going to be with the same people all your life, and funnily enough a lot of these guys stuck together for a long time as this way of life wasn't a fad, it was what they had been waiting for, because it was relaxed and less competitive. Because I was competitive, and good at most things, I always thought that was the way everything should be. How mistaken I was, only ever seeing my own point of view.

I hit the club scene, everyone driving up to clubs in Liverpool, Manchester and further afield. Before I knew it I was getting full of drink and tablets, and all kinds of pills and potions. The club scene wasn't for me; it wasn't even proper dancing! Before long I became frustrated and was getting mashed on drugs and drinking heavily, 10 to 15 pints every time I went out, getting into fights, then having to be looked after.

Even when the college term started, nothing changed. I was now renowned in my home town for being an idiot, just wanting to battle with everyone, even turning on my own friends sometimes. I

would get into trouble at college time after time, until eventually I was thrown out.

I worked with my dad for a short while before leaving to find work on a building site. I also got done for assault, although in all fairness that one wasn't my fault. I was no longer a part of the gang I had been around for so long; I was only now tolerated because of the past and how things used to be. The truth was, the gym was only round the corner, I could have gone there at any time, but I think I missed school, the way things were, and I just kept hoping that somehow things would go back to being that way again. Of course, that didn't happen, and unfortunately there would have to be a death amongst us before I would finally change my ways and move on to the next part of my life.

That night started the same as all the rest, with everyone in the club dancing about, doing their own thing. I don't remember much about that night; all I remember is seeing police and paramedics gathered round the place where we had all been sitting, but not much else. I remember being told something had happened to Allie, a friend at the time. That he had collapsed after taking Ecstasy, first time he had taken it, but I went home not knowing much more than that. The following day I got a phone call saying Allie had died.

Later that week, some of the lads who had been out that night went to see Allie's parents, to send their regards, they said that from this they had learnt a lesson, and that out of respect for Allie they were going to change their ways. When the weekend came this was relayed back to everyone. I was elated, thinking that everything was going to change for the better, but within a week it was back to square one, with everyone back on the drugs, ready to set off to some big rave once more. When I turned up at our usual weekend meeting point, and asked what was going on, one of the lads just said "It's what Allie would have wanted; he would have wanted us to carry on partying!" I'd never heard such bullshit in all my life, and after all the crap they had told Allie's parents only the week before.

I knew at that point that nothing was going to change. My childlike notion that we were all going to live our lives like they did on the TV series Neighbours, everyone close and sharing their problems, this idea now seemed ridiculous. I didn't go out with them that night, nor would I go out with them ever again. There would never be a bigger wake up call, telling me now was the time to pursue my dream. As I turned away that night I never looked back.

THERE WOULD NEVER BE A BIGGER WAKE UP CALL, TELLING ME NOW WAS THE TIME TO PURSUE MY DREAM. AS I TURNED AWAY THAT NIGHT I NEVER LOOKED BACK.

basically I was doing
everything I could to keep
me away from my old life

CHAPTER 4

From death comes a new start

It felt as if I had to restart my life from scratch. First I joined the gym, and then I managed to get onto an apprenticeship in mechanical engineering, but I couldn't get a placement with any engineering companies so I had to do my first year as a mechanic working at a local garage. I worked as a glass collector at the church social club, and then me and my pal Porky joined the Royal Fusiliers army regiment, part time; basically I was doing everything I could to keep me away from my old life. After finishing at the gym I would usually play football with some of the younger lads, before going home for my tea. I filled my days well.

I had now constructed my first real diet. I'd have two raw eggs and Weetabix for breakfast, then a load of tuna sandwiches spread throughout the day. After I'd done my training I'd have a massive protein shake made with whole milk, two raw eggs and two bananas, followed by a flapjack. For tea I'd have two big jackets, cottage cheese and tuna, which would take me over an hour to eat every night.

I got Rob, the gym-owner, to sort me out a training plan. Rob was the current Mr Universe, the first world champion bodybuilder ever to come out of Bury, he was the man. Before joining the gym, I had tried talking to him once when in town with my mates. He just stared at me, not saying a word; my mates all laughed and said, "He looked like he really likes you… in the way he just ignored you." We laughed about it afterwards, but still this guy was awesome, he looked like The Terminator, and even though he didn't speak much I knew that was the look I wanted. Wherever that guy was training, that's where I was going.

THIS GUY WAS AWESOME, HE LOOKED LIKE THE TERMINATOR, AND EVEN THOUGH HE DIDN'T SPEAK MUCH I KNEW THAT WAS THE LOOK I WANTED. WHEREVER THAT GUY WAS TRAINING, THAT'S WHERE I WAS GOING.

CHAPTER 5

Silver's gym

My first impression of Silver's was not what I had expected. In the foyer everyone sat at tables, and seemed to know and like each other well. Rob was sat at one of the tables, he asked if I was all right, then just said, "Are you doing a session?" He had a big smile on his face, I just nodded before turning towards the counter. I actually felt star-struck when he spoke, but the fact that he looked like a cyborg still made me feel a little unnerved. I spoke to the lady behind the counter. She was a lovely woman who made me feel instantly welcome; she had a big smile, and made polite conversation. She showed me where everything was, then told me to enjoy my session. This turned out to be Rob's mum, Maureen.

There were no windows from the foyer to the gym, so when you got inside the training area and the door had closed the atmosphere immediately changed. Everybody was grunting and sweating, the weights piled up on every machine, some of the guys had purple faces, and everyone looked like a pro to me at this time. My first memory was a guy they called Sarge (David Rowlands), he was under the lifting rack squatting a massive amount of weight, he had a guy behind him keeping him steady. The weights were clanging together, with a bar that looked to be bending, his face was purple, with steam coming off his back. When he put the weights down a few of the lads patted him on the back, to kind of pay him respect for the amount of weight he had just squatted.

Everyone had an intense look about them and was going to the wire; I couldn't wait to get started and have that look. I didn't get off to the best start. I saw a guy with really big arms, his name Roger

Bentley. He looked friendly enough, and was training with a guy that I knew a little, so I went over to speak. "What do you do to get your arms so big?" I said. "Arm exercises," he replied, sarcastically. As he walked away, laughing, I lost my rag and called him a dickhead. His pal tried to calm me down, saying Roger was just having a laugh and for me to wind my neck in. It turned out that Roger was a sound lad, this was gym banter, this kind of sarcasm something I would have to get used to.

As I started training I decided to turn up the radio, but within minutes a big black guy, his name Paul Clarke, came through looking furious, saw me and said "Keep it down!" whilst turning the radio down himself. It felt as if everyone in the gym was glaring at me. I pretty much shit myself as, a year or so earlier, I had come off my skateboard when in town and my board had hit this same guy in his shin! The big guy had picked my board up, and launched it at me, with me running for my life in the other direction. I kept my head down but kept on training, just hoping he didn't remember me, and for a while I decided to leave the radio alone.

> *"What do you do to get your arms so big?" I said. "Arm exercises," he replied, sarcastically.*

As 1990 turned into 1991 I had put on a decent amount of weight, and I was training hard. I could now see straight; initially the withdrawal from going out all the time had affected me more than I thought it would have. I'm not saying I was drug fucked or anything but for the first four or five months after I stopped going out I used to get bad headaches that would last for days, I'd feel clammy and sometimes disorientated, I was glad I got out of that life when I did.

The kids I took playing football had nowhere to go during the winter, so I spoke to the local priest with him agreeing to open up the church hall so I could start a youth club. Because the big kids were beating up the little kids, we had Sunday night for the older end and Monday night for the younger. The older kids were more my age group, and a few of them were into bodybuilding so before long they had become friends. This was my first step back into some kind of social structure. I still wasn't quite myself, but I was on the right path. The road to bodybuilding would need a set structure; that's what I now had.

Gym life was good, and even though I had to put up with the sarcastic banter I had learned to give it back

Gym life was good, and even though I had to put up with the sarcastic banter I had learned to give it back and was no longer intimidated by the bigger, scarier members of the gym. I would ask a lot of questions, trying to learn more about my chosen sport. The likes of Sarge, Big Ste Harrison, Phil Barber and Paul Clarke would always give their time, and proper answers, as they could see I was trying hard. These guys turned out to be the salt-of-the-earth if they liked you, but if they didn't and in any way you decided to wrong the gym it would have been a different matter! I had seen them rapping a guy's knuckles with a weight, he had been caught stealing from the gym, and on another occasion I had seen them hanging a guy by his ankles over the wall outside, which was around three storeys up, for reasons I never found out. I was pretty glad they liked me.

Even a big guy by the name of Andy McKenzie (the North West's strong man champion) who had terrified me early-doors, would actually start to warm to me a little, but he had the scariest laugh I had ever heard, and would still stare at me like he wanted to kill me even when I thought we were getting on OK. Some of the other guys I would hear laughing behind my back, talking about me like I was a laughing stock. I vowed then that if I ever got good enough to have people asking me for advice, I would always take time out for them, and to this day I always have.

Mr Bury 91. Top row left to right: Me,
Matt Warren, Anne Spavrin,
Louise Fletcher, Pete, Ben
McDermott. Front: Heidi Roberts,
Dave Jones

CHAPTER 6

Mr Bury 91-92 The learning curve

Rob had noted I'd put on some size, he told me he was running a local show and asked if I would be interested. I was really happy that he thought me good enough to do a show, and although very nervous I agreed and thanked him. This was where my bodybuilding career would start.

My preparation for the Mr Bury '91 was now to begin. I started my diet about eight weeks out from the contest; I remember it consisting of mainly chicken and rice. I didn't know the difference between basmati, long grain, wholegrain, low-GI or essential fats; in fact I didn't know much about anything when it came to my first diet. I even thought that fried chicken was OK as long as you took the skin off, and that all the fat was in the skin! I had made a few errors so by four weeks to go I was falling behind with my prep.

Rob put me on a tuna/chicken and grapefruit diet, which was just what it said on the tin! I stuck to the diet but it was too little too late; I was still quite fat as well as holding water with the lack of calories leaving my muscle looking deflated. As the contest drew nearer, there were some improvements. I could visibly see my chest, the thickness of my traps and back, and just how much muscle I'd actually put on (although I was still wondering when my abs were going to arrive as they were only a faint outline at this point!) with the concept of eating-up off-season, and then dieting down for a contest still leaving me puzzled. My idea of bodybuilding was still relative to the '70s, where a lot of the bodybuilders competed fuller, without as much detail – in other words, they weren't massively ripped. Stupidly, I ended up listening to an out-of-shape idiot to put my mind at ease. He said my muscle was still young and that by next year my fat would have turned into muscle; he said I was in pretty good shape, that I had nothing to worry about. Good advice was essential come contest time, someone trying to build your confidence wasn't always the best thing.

The day had arrived, it was time to meet the competition. As we went inside the venue, which was the local night club, I looked for people around my age, trying to find out who would be in my line-up. I knew one lad from our gym but figured I had him beat – although in reasonable condition, he was a bit too slim to be of a threat.

> *I could only look in disbelief, quickly accepting that I could only get third place, but at least I would get a trophy.*

Before long we were called backstage to pump up, this being where the bodybuilder uses weights and press-ups to force blood into the muscles. This makes the muscle appear at its fullest and most vascular. There were four in my class, and I was happy because at first glance and with our shirts still on, I looked to be the biggest. But as the shirts came off, everything changed. One of the lads was only quite small but he had amazing condition. The other lad, I couldn't believe was even our age. His name was Ian Harrison (not the pro by the same name). He looked like Slider out of Top Gun, with massive vascular arms and shoulders, and amazing dryness (this meaning he didn't look to be holding any kind of moisture beneath his skin). I could only look in disbelief, quickly accepting that I could only get third place, but at least I would get a trophy.

As we all walked on stage I instantly felt the buzz of competition, I would be getting compared like the guys in (the bodybuilding documentary) Pumping Iron. There was only a small audience in the afternoon, as most people would be arriving in the evening, but I posed on with great excitement, enjoying my first taste of being on stage.

After coming off stage we would have to stick around for the night show. When I had got ready, heading back out to the front, I noticed Karl Bleakley and Big Lee Martin sat at the back of the venue, so went over to speak to them. Karl was a good guy, he had always given me the time of day, he was always complimentary. He had recently competed, and although the underdog, he had made it to a UK Final. Lee, on the other hand, was 'the next big thing', very popular, with loads of potential. He worked at the gym and was also a local doorman; he was sometimes sarcastic but quite funny with it.

I asked Lee how I looked, he just replied "Smooth." I took this as a compliment at the time, thinking he meant 'smooth' like Pierce Brosnan (James Bond). As it turned out he meant 'smooth' like a dolphin's head – a nice way of saying I was still pretty fat.

The night show commenced. The show had great support from the gym with everyone's family and friends coming to watch the show. My whole family had turned up, including both my sisters, as well as a couple of cousins. I no longer had the morning jitters so was looking forward to going back on stage for the final pose-down.

For the last time we all went on stage, all going head to head, flexing to the max. In my head I was Arnold, I was buzzing, I knew this was my sport, with the stage the place I wanted to be. The final placing came in, as we all lined up ready to hear the result. Third place was announced, but to my horror it wasn't me; the slender kid from the gym had beaten me. Right away my heart sank, then within moments I felt the heat of shame on my face, even tears now building behind my eyes. I wanted to try to make light of it, but just

froze lifelessly. I was stranded, my face saying a thousand words, with the audience now reading it too.

That couple of minutes felt like forever. As we finally walked off stage I could feel my head banging, and my heart pounding. I quickly got ready and left via the fire-door, not even able to face my own family. As I lay in bed that night my mind was in overdrive, worrying about what people would think. My friends who looked up to me, the lads down the gym, how upset I had looked on stage, all the changes I'd put in place, every bodybuilding memory now sour in my mind.

I didn't get much sleep that night but still, by the morning, my mind was made up. There was only one real answer; get back to the gym, train harder, and most importantly make sure I turned up in shape next time.

As the week went by I got a call asking me to come down to the gym to have a photo taken for the local newspaper. I was a little reluctant, but knew I had to face the music sooner or later (and I didn't want to miss out on having my picture in the paper!). As I walked into the gym, Big Lee looked up with a smile on his face. "How are you?" he asked. "Good, thanks," I said.

Then other gym members started coming in, asking how I was, actually being more pleasant to me than usual. I realised that these guys were a lot more human than they had let on. The arguments and sarcastic vibe of the gym was more about character building, only in place to get a rise from me, no one actually liked seeing me beat. I stood for the picture, not knowing that it was going to turn things around in my already flagging bodybuilding career.

As the paper dropped through the door on Friday morning I was quick to get a grip of it, turning straight to the page that the picture was on – and was instantly very happy with what I saw. The picture didn't really show what type of shape I'd been in, it just showed the fullness and shape of the muscle, leaving me looking biggest on the page. I was pretty made-up with it, but this was just the start.

The local kids from the youth clubs, as well as my neighbours, congratulated me, thinking I had won. Even when I put them right, they still said that I had looked the best. When I saw my friends, even though I told them the outcome, I didn't elaborate on how I'd felt at the show, only my plans on winning it next time. The shop where I bought fruit gave me a regular discount and put the picture up on the back wall, and even though I didn't know much, people started asking me for training advice.

The success of the show had got the neighbouring gym, Derby's, talking. They were already forming a team of young upcoming bodybuilders, my name regularly being mentioned as the man they were out to beat. I'd looked shit and come last, but obviously none of the Derby's crowd had been to watch the show, so had based everything on the one picture, thinking I'd done better than I actually had. But regardless of how I actually went on or how I looked, I was going to live up to the perceived reputation they had of me, so was ready to rise to the challenge. In fact the only place I didn't have a good reputation was my own gym; I think I was pretty much a write-off at this time.

1992 had arrived with things looking up. I had my entourage of local friends who were all into bodybuilding. Our walls were all plastered with bodybuilding pictures from the magazines; Francis Benfatto, Lee Labrada, Bob Paris, Porter Cottrell and Shawn Ray, to mention but a few. I was constantly watching the Olympia videos from 90-91, already a big fan of the aesthetic, symmetrical look, the condition and proportions of these guys was outstanding. This was the look I wanted and was now working for. My '70s notion of bodybuilding was well and truly forgotten. I'd watched these videos so often that even my eight-year-old sister

> *When I went back to the gym the following Monday hardly anyone recognised me, so I knew I was on the right track!*

knew the names and placing of all the competitors in them. I even named my cat after one of the bodybuilders, calling her Berry de Mog, after the bodybuilder Berry de Mey.

The bodybuilding season was back and I had decided to diet early this time, and had even decided to go away for three weeks of army training, as I thought this would be the best and quickest way to get the fat off. I'd been in the army part-time for over a year, doing a lot of my basic training over various weekends, but the time had come to do my 'card', this making me a fully trained fusilier. There would be three weeks away, that's three weeks of hard training, coming back at the start of August for another nine weeks of training to take me up to the show. This was going to be tough, but I was going to be up on that stage in superb condition no matter what I had to go through to get there.

I cleaned up my diet four to five weeks before going away, only eating tuna and rice. Before I went off to do my army training I had already lost six pounds, which give me a head start, but still when the army training started my fitness was not what I hoped it would be. Although I looked massive in comparison to the others, for the first couple of days I was flagging in the running, falling behind, but by the end of the week my weight had dropped some, with my fitness starting to shine through.

The main aim of doing the army training was to drop some weight – but being competitive I wanted to make my mark. Before long I was staying up with the better runners and, as the training increased, we were soon running with back-packs and rifles, with me now finishing top of the grid. I set the best time for the assault course, was most accurate at the shooting. I even held my breath the longest in the gas-chamber test. Overall it was an experience and a challenge all of its own, and one I got through with flying colours, placing third out of forty, receiving my feather and soldier status.

It was my 18th birthday during that training course, and it turned out I was the only guy who turned up on their birthday to do the training so I got a reward for my commitment – I was given a chance to go on a double-bladed helicopter, the kind where you had your feet on the landing pads, like in the movie Predator. The other guys had to draw straws for the privilege. I celebrated that night, even had a few drinks and got into a bit of trouble, it was a good day and the last celebration I would have, as on getting back I knew it would be time for Round Two.

After the military training, I was totally transformed. My big pale face was now tanned and lean, topped with a short cropped hair cut. I had dropped nearly 20 pounds in total, so was already looking lean. When I went back to the gym the following Monday hardly anyone recognised me, so I knew I was on the right track! I started with my diet right away; grapefruit and chicken five times a day, every day.

The Mr Bury '92 was drawing closer, and the fact I had been so quiet meant not many people knew I was competing. I had kept fully-clothed and out of sight for the most time. I would practice my routines in the side rooms with friends Anne and Karl, also this is where Rob would keep an eye on my condition.

From Silver's, the favourite for the 18-and-unders was a lad named Chris; he had big arms and shoulders with a lot of people saying he was like a young Arnold. He was seeking advice from the bigger fish so always did his posing in the main gym with everyone looking on. The main story was the under-21s competitor Lee Martin, aka Big Lee. He was training for the Junior Britain but was going to do the Bury show as a stop-off on the way. Lee already looked like a young pro so was getting most of the attention at the gym. I had kept out of the spotlight at our gym but across town I had three young up-comers wanting to take me down. I was told that John Latham (who was my equivalent age-wise and size-wise) was going to be there, and was shouting-off about beating me, as well as two younger up-comers, Phil and Roger, who were said to be super-dedicated and already in shape. The two trained together, with both wanting the title, so now I knew I had my work cut out.

I was around four weeks in, and starting to feel it. My skin looked grey and my face gaunt. My gums were looking like a half-drained cup lolly, because of all the grapefruit I'd had to eat, and my ability to function was at an all-time low. My training wasn't affected – I think my brain was so tired it didn't have the energy to tell my body it couldn't lift, so I just carried on. With my cardio, I would be speed-marching one minute, then on my arse the next, no warning; luckily I would have my crew to pick me up and make sure I got home OK, they seemed to think this was cool.

At work, assembling and testing machines, I was starting to struggle. One day I was sent to the boss's office after falling asleep on one of the machines I was supposed to be watching. I swore blind I didn't, but unfortunately the machine had been quite hot, and had left a bar-like burn across my forehead. No one thought to tell me about it, they just let me carry on swearing blind I hadn't. It wasn't until catching a look in the mirror, I realised just how much of a dong I had made of myself; quite funny looking back now.

I managed to survive another couple of weeks, but ten days before the show, I hit a wall. I could no longer focus on my workout, everything seemed dark, I was disorientated. I decided to speak to Rob about my tiredness, telling him how I was. Rob was very understanding, he took me to one side then said quietly, "John, go home, get yourself a big bowl of porridge and three to four whole eggs." This didn't sound like no miracle cure to me. If Rob hadn't been following the same diet, and looking equally as crazy, I would have sworn he had it in for me. My only logic at this time was that Rob was doing it, and he was the best, so I'd do it and be at my best.

> *I could no longer focus on my workout, everything seemed dark, I was disorientated.*

So that night I went home to eat my porridge and eggs, not quite sure of what effect it was going to have, if any. On eating the porridge I felt instantly relaxed, so decided to have an early night, and for the first time in a long time I fell into a deep sleep. When I woke the next morning my head was pumping full of blood, I felt very much alive, also very hungry. As I took my morning ritual look in the mirror I could see, but couldn't believe, what that one meal and the night's sleep had done. My body looked like a 3D road map with veins shooting everywhere, my metabolism now racing. In the next three to four days I would be exactly where I wanted to be.

By the Tuesday I knew I was ready, the pick-me-up had left me in top shape, shredded. I had kept the promise I had made to myself the year earlier, I now looked my very best, and more importantly had done my very best, this was it.

My friends wanted to watch the show, but with the past year still looming in my mind, I made excuses for them not to come. I knew this show could make or break me. Last year I hadn't looked my best, but this year I couldn't have looked any better and if I was about to get another bad outcome, what might look like a new beginning could easily be the beginning of the end, taking my new-found confidence with it.

The day of the Mr Bury 92 arrived and I found myself back in my least favourite venue. I didn't speak to many people, and arrived wearing baggy jeans and a sweater in order not to bring attention to myself, just sat out of the way, waiting for the call back. When it came I went into the toilets where everyone was getting ready, the whole of the class was already stripped down, oiling up. I stood at the side before stripping off. Within moments all eyes were on me, I was now looked at in the same way Ian Harrison had been last year when doing the same class. The young lads from Derby's came over to introduce themselves, then one of them just said, "I think you've got it", in a defeated type manner. Chris hadn't lived up to expectations, but the two lads from Derby's certainly had. John Latham had dropped out, and there was a young lad named Damien Lees who had come in ill-prepared, similar to me the year earlier.

It was now show time and onto the stage we all went for the comparisons. As I walked on stage I could see faces from last year, some of them looked surprised to see me, and even more surprised to see me in shape. I was in the first call-out and had taken centre-stage, this was a good sign; then in the second, I was then asked to stand back as the other guys were compared. I didn't get another call-out so as I came off stage I thought I'd won – I wasn't 100% sure, but knew I was definitely in the top three.

The night show soon came around, the place was packed. I now wished I'd told my friends to come, but I had only brought my immediate family. All the Derby's crowd had turned up, and I think virtually everyone from our gym had shown up to watch too. Rob made a brief announcement, before calling us all on stage. The usually quietly-spoken Rob was now blazing our names out as we came on, shouting to the crowd to get behind us. The crowd was roaring as we went through our last lot of compulsory poses. As the pose-down was announced I could now hear that most of the crowd was for me, even people I barely knew were shouting. It was all such a massive rush, I didn't want it to end, fighting for this title meant everything, it had felt great to have come back having given it my all, but as the music faded we were called off stage to await the verdict for the final three.

The final three were announced. It was me, Roger and Phil, the two young lads from Derby's. Phil was placed for third, so it was now between me and Roger. The nerves hit for a second, but then hearing Roger's name in second place I instantly hit an all-time high. I'd won my very first victory, and in front of my home crowd. It was only a town's show, but with how I was, you would have thought I'd won the Mr Universe. I felt like I had been lit up for all to see. This, my first great bodybuilding moment.

Before I came off stage Rob made the announcement and said, "John competed here last year and has come back very much improved with this show in mind, and has taken the title. Well done John!" I felt proud Rob had noticed how hard I had worked. That night I walked out of my favourite venue a different person, now knowing the sky was the limit.

The competitive season carried on with more success. I bagged an area title, as well as the 17-18s segment, and a 3rd in the Junior UK, I was now on the map. I realised the bad experience I'd had in '91 wasn't a setback, it was what actually made me come back fighting so hard in this year. I didn't feel it right just to move on without coming back to win the Mr Bury, just as I hadn't thought it right not to come back to do the chin-up event when at school.

It took me a lot of guts to come back and fight for this title, especially after the embarrassing beating I had taken the year before. I believe that once you start accepting loss as the norm it will eventually consume who you are, taking a lot of your self-belief with it. This was the reason I always came back, I would always want to finish what I started and with no regrets.

For the rest of the competitors that night, Lee brought the house down and went on to win the junior British championships a couple of weeks later (with Karl winning the most unhappy man award for having to be on stage next to him!). Roger and Phil fell out shortly after the contest, never to compete again, and Chris never did become the next Arnold. But young Damian Lees, who finished last that year, took the bull by the horns, going on to become world class several years down the line. John Latham, my rival at the time, used to say that he wouldn't have beat me but would have come in a close second if he had competed, this I find funny as he still says it, even to present day.

> *over time I became the voice of knowledge and knowhow throughout the gym when it came to nutrition and training advice*

After the season was over I formed an unlikely friendship with Big Lee who had fallen on hard times. He was facing dismissal from work after not following a security procedure, this had come at the same time he was prepping for the Junior Universe, he wasn't able to focus so ended up not taking part. Lee and I used to run into each other pretty regularly. I would wish him the best, we would talk about bodybuilding, but more about our futures in the sport, just to take his mind off the present. Eventually Lee got to keep his job, so with a seemingly solid bodybuilding future in front of him he was able to put the disappointment of the Universe contest to the back of his mind.

1992 moved into 1993. I was still active in both youth clubs but the older end club was more segregated, with me, Mark Holt (Holty), Mark Thomson (Tommo) and Z (these lads being the ones I had grown close to whilst competing over the past couple of years) now hanging as more of a group. Z and Holty were regularly training with me at the gym. I'd finished with the army, so gym life was rapidly becoming my world. I'd finished my time in engineering, with no remote interest in it. Shortly after I left, then got a job as a postman. It seemed to be the job for bodybuilders at the time with Roger, Lee, Karl and Holty also working as mail men. At home, my dad and I seemed to keep having fall-outs, mainly due to a clash of personalities, and it didn't help that I was eating them out of house and home either. I eventually would have to leave.

Not knowing what to do when I first left, I ended up sleeping under a tree for the first couple of days! I had my sports bag, which was full of cans of tuna and wholegrain bread. I never missed a meal, or a training session, my Aunty Doreen then let me rent her old house. The house was great, there wasn't much in it, but I didn't need much anyway and even though it was close to where a lot of the local drug addicts lived, I never witnessed any problems whilst stopping there. This house would be the centre for my education as a body builder.

I was given ten books on training and nutrition given by my pal Roger Bentley, as well as purchasing my very first copy of the Encyclopaedia of Modern Bodybuilding. I was a very slow and quite a poor reader and would sometimes have to copy down words I didn't understand for Tommo to tell me what they said and meant. I know not being able to read and write very well is usually related to not being very intelligent, but although it took me nearly two years to get through only ten books, by the end I had remembered everything, so over time I became the voice of knowledge and knowhow throughout the gym when it came to nutrition and training advice. I had no TV with only a radio for company, which was good, as it kept me focused, keeping my head in the books.

I had two main mentors in this year – both would educate me, but in different ways. The first and most informative would be Barny. When he came on the scene he took me under his wing more or less right away. He was a Junior British Champion, but was now competing in the 70kg class for the Natural UK. I went along to watch him in his shows; he never seemed tired, and would explain every step of the way for every contest he did. He had charts, graphs, diaries, and was very courteous when it came to giving his time. I would bring note pads to the gym, jotting everything down he was telling me. Sometimes, when he became over-scientific, I would ask him to break things down for me to understand, which he did, and not only would he know what to do, he could prove it worked with his success in contests. In this year he won both regional and UK titles, as well as finishing third at the Britain; removing any question about his advice on bodybuilding and diet.

The other guy who helped me was Big Lee Martin. Lee had a more common sense approach to bodybuilding, he knew a lot about genetics and how the muscle should look. He explained a lot about aesthetics and symmetry. We talked about different body types, he also knew quite a lot about the who's who on the pro scene, educating me on who had won what and when. I enjoyed our talks whilst walking home from the gym, the sunny evenings I remember fondly. Lee also taught me something I'd long forgotten; how to have fun!

Training was going great, with my strength on most things going through the roof, racking up a 150kg bench-press, 180kg dead-lift, as well as shoulder-pressing the 40kg dumbbells. I stayed closer in shape this year, varying my diet throughout. I felt and looked great, and with my victories in tow, my ego was growing even quicker than my muscles. Lee and I started hanging out, and before long we became almost like a duo. Our banter had the whole gym laughing, everyone joining in, and with both our training and contest records now skying, we also had a certain amount of respect around the gym. We became well known around town, and in the pubs and clubs we went, we would usually get in free, always well greeted wherever we went.

Because of our daft confidence, good looks and carefree ways we had no shortage of female admirers, and seemed to have pick of the litter when in town or on nights out. I enjoyed every day, from working in the morning, to being in the gym at dinner, to hanging out in town, to my quiet time alone at night reading and educating myself. I did compete that year, but only placed third in the under-21s, training up to the event with both Holty and my pal Chris Whitehead. It wasn't a problem though, as I saw that particular year as more experimental, trying to find out what worked and what didn't. I mainly hung with Lee but had growing friendships with Barny, Karl Bleakly and a young up-comer by the name of Matt Thomson.

Mr Bury 1992, first place

Lee Martin: Junior British Champion 1992

CHAPTER 7

As the heroes start to fall

1994 started out pretty much the same as the year before, but with a big off-season coming up, and no contests planned for the whole year, I was looking forward to getting some bulk on. My life had recently become all about the gym. The council at the youth clubs had voted me off the committee, saying that the kids looked up to me, but saw me as a friend, and the elders were finding it hard to instil health and safety with me doing what I wanted. I had started the youth clubs, taking the kids collecting wood for bonfires, playing football, skateboarding, earning the trust of all the parents in the neighbourhood, but politics won and I was gone. Within a year of me leaving, both clubs had closed down, leaving the kids back out on the streets where they had started, that's the law for you.

Big Lee was now at his biggest, he was 21 stone with 22-inch arms, and was looking forward to competing later this year. Unfortunately this wouldn't happen as tragedy would strike him once more. He got into a fight whilst working the door, and had been hit by a steel bar, shattering his arm. His arm was put back together with steel rods and pins, but he was left with an inch-thick scar going all the way down his arm. Despite this, his confidence didn't seem rocked, and he was soon back in the weight room once more. Even though competing was out of the question for the year, Lee soon filled back out and was already talking about next year's season.

Everything had returned to normal and we even took a holiday break as now none of us were competing. We got back from holiday and had started hanging out as usual, but no sooner had Lee started to see the light, he was out of the game once more. If breaking his arm wasn't serious enough he now had suffered a strangulated double hernia, which was potentially life threatening. I didn't get to see Lee for the best part of a week when it first happened, and when I did see him he was in a hospital bed. We made small talk when I first walked in, then for some reason there was a kind of awkward silence, then Lee just said, "I don't think I'll be squatting for a while," and just the way he said it made me think that this could be the end for Big Lee. With how he looked at me, I knew he thought the same. As I left the room that day, my heart sank, and that night I prayed for things to be OK for him, I saw his situation as if I was going through it myself. The next couple of times I went up to see him I tried to use humour to get through the visits, sometimes using the gas mask that was at the side of his bed as a cod piece, singing Cameo songs, or doing daft Top Gun scenes. Everyone would laugh, apart from his mum who I think was more worried about Lee's stitches bursting.

Apart from my worries for Lee, everything to do with training was going well, I even took on the might of Phil and Big Ste. These two were the most powerful guys in the gym; they were very sarcastic, but sincere characters who loved the banter but loved the training more. I wasn't reaching my goals, especially on legs, so when I told them, they were both happy and willing to put me through the wall to help me reach them. Gym sessions with them were a step up from anything I was used to, and during legs I would often bottom out on squats trying to make my 150kg goal. I worked beyond my capabilities and would regularly suffer burst blood vessels in my eyes, monster nose bleeds, not to mention the vomiting and dizziness during or after the workouts. After four to five months I had reached all my goals. I was squatting 150kg, dead-lifting 200kg as well as flat-benching 150kg. I had also got up to my intended weight of 14 stone, so the big lads had definitely done their job. The hard core training carried on, and I teamed up for the rest of the year with intense training partner Assim Uddin.

Lee was now out of hospital and back at the gym, he was out of danger and on good form. I had put on some size and Lee noticed. He also noticed a lot of it was on my backside through squatting – I had developed quite a booty! As I was walking to the counter at the gym, I just heard the words, "Hey, bread bin arse," then a roar of laughter from everyone sat in the foyer. I went bright red, then laughed; Lee was back, and the banter with him, with the rest of the year playing out as it had started.

As the next year breezed in I was looking forward to my competitive season, aiming for the British Championships in the Junior Under-21s section. Over the course of the year myself and Lee would drift apart; he became caught up with work, then later in the same year he bought a house and settled down with a girl he had met when we had been on a night out. I, on the other hand, would only be caught up with the gym.

My friendship with Matt had grown as I'd helped him prepare for his shows, spending a lot of time round his house. He was the first top competitor I would get ready, start to end. Matt was hard to work with as he never spoke much, he used to strip off every 10 to 15 minutes to look at himself and kept asking if he was still in good condition. I found this kind of strange because he was absolutely shredded; he was mostly blank-looking, expressionless at times and would regularly stop talking mid-conversation, almost like his brain had ran out of batteries. Nevertheless he had a good season, and would help me out also when it came to mine, we became good friends.

In the same year I had managed to win over the mighty Rob. We had always had a 'hot-and-cold' friendship. I'd embarrassed him in the past with a story which involved a two-way mirror, Rob rolling his pants up and flexing his legs while people were still working inside, one of them (unfortunately for Rob) being my mum. I thought it would make him laugh, but he just flipped out, not seeing the funny side at all. I could also be a bit crude sometimes. Bad language was the norm around the gym but if I used it while his mum was working there, it didn't sit well with him. I was a bit young and daft, to be fair. But by this point I had now realised the errors of my ways and once I started being more careful about what I was saying, myself and Rob would start getting along well.

Rob asked me, along with his main training partner who was also named John, to train with him up to the Mr Britain; what an honour, if this was rock'n'roll it would be like touring with Elvis! He even included me in his magazine photo shoot with the famous photographer Roger Shelley. Most importantly, he went on to win the Britain that year so I was really happy to have been included, I had really enjoyed being a part of it all.

I was competing again myself. I'd won my regional qualifier so was now getting ready for the British final. I'd devised my own diet plan this time, but no matter what I did, I couldn't seem to get into the same shape as I had done for the town's show three years earlier. I couldn't work it out, I was doing everything right and to the book. My legs, back and arms were quite tight, but my abs and chest would have looked more at home on a beach than on a stage. This was something I would have to sort out in the future.

I had spent ten weeks preparing for this show but in truth I was still only in the learning stages of trying to find out what worked best (as well as what didn't), and it could sometimes be frustrating.

I was now ready to do my first British Championship. I found out that there was only four in my class, and since my aim was to make the top five, I had nothing to worry about. Or did I? When I went to sign in, I handed over my birth certificate, and the official told me I couldn't compete! I was 21 and the category was strictly under-21s, not 21-and-under like most Federations. My junior career ended here, I was gutted. After all that hard work I was no further up the ladder than I had been three years earlier.

The thought of not competing at a national level just kept eating away at me, I knew I couldn't just leave it, I hadn't trained and dieted all this time just to go home. I heard about a Natural Novice UK contest, it wouldn't be until the early part of the following year which wasn't ideal, but I was going to go for it so started my assault right away. Initially it was good getting right back at it as the gym was buzzing. Rob had won the Britain (British champion) and was training for his pro card in the Grand Prix; there were big name bodybuilders all over the gym who were part of Rob's sponsorship team, as well as others just coming down to train or chat, with the most noted of them being a lad named John Hodgson.

> *The thought of not competing at a national level just kept eating away at me, I knew I couldn't just leave it*

John and I would train together a couple of times a week. He was mad for it just like I was, he was very complimentary towards me, telling me I was the best natural bodybuilder he had ever seen. He was extremely focused on the things he wanted to achieve and tended to say things as they were. His physique would always look full, and for me, John and a guy named Paul George would be the bench marks, possibly the two best conditioned guys in the country, Paul in the 70/75kg class, and John in the 80kg class, both British champions.

When John had something to say, he would literally be in the moment. I remember him driving us up to a show. As we pulled into the car park, John was talking, and he was looking at me. He drove into a wall but didn't stop talking. It wasn't until he had made his point that he snapped back into the real world, and said, "Did I just hit that wall?" It was kind of scary but funny at the same time. I could tell by his attitude that he was destined for great things, so it came as no shock when years down the line he made it big in the pro ranks, taking runner-up at some of the big shows, I even think he made the final 6 at the Mr Olympia 202 class, I know he definitely made the top ten. In his final show, the British Grand Prix, he placed second to the one and only Flex Louis. John looked phenomenal, by far his best, a great way for him to leave the sport.

On this year I would be lucky enough to train with John, Rob and Matt, the cream of British bodybuilding at the time. Asked by name, as I would always put in a good workout, this to me was an honour.

I was stoked for Rob as he was on the back of the pro career he had always wanted, there looked to be no stopping him; I wish it had been the case. I was in the foyer when Rob came out of the gym holding the side of his chest, with John and another guy assisting him. He told them he was OK and for some reason he went over to the sink, then I heard some plates smash on the floor. Rob was stooped over. I rushed to help him and a few of us got him sat down. As I spoke to Rob to see if he was OK, I saw the same look I had seen in Lee's eyes only a year earlier, I now sensed the worse. After a couple of days we were told Rob had suffered a pec tear, a detachment from his chest to his shoulder. He wouldn't be in the gym for a while.

By the end of the year I had barely seen Rob, in fact not many people had, so I decided to pay him a surprise visit on Christmas Eve. Rob and his mum Maureen were glad to see me when I turned up at the house, both making me feel very welcome. It was the first time on a Christmas Eve I had thought of someone other than myself, and I was glad I had. We had a whisky as we brought in Christmas, I felt pleased I had made the effort.

Rob Worthington and John Hodgson winning the British 1995 – Matt on the left, me on the right.

I WOULD BE LUCKY ENOUGH TO TRAIN WITH JOHN, ROB AND MATT, THE CREAM OF BRITISH BODYBUILDING AT THE TIME.

My mind-set of not giving up
was still in place

CHAPTER 8

Reality bites and self doubt takes over

From the start of the year I was already dieting for my upcoming show as well as getting Matt ready for his starting season. When it came to Matt I would always do my best, knowing how seriously he took the sport. This year he was looking fantastic: thick, full, tight, amazing V taper, and with legs like you wouldn't believe. He had a great season, bagging an overall regional title as well as taking the Super-Heavyweight and overall UK; he was misplaced in the British but still managed a solid third.

When it came to my own career I didn't seem able to put a foot right. I think because of the difficult hard-hitting off-season, and an overly long competitive season, my body had become nonresponsive, over-tired and over-worked. My mind-set of not giving up was still in place, but unlike earlier contests where I had come back fighting it now seemed more like I was just trying to get over the line.

The day came to compete, with me as ready as my body would let me be, but my usual buzz to get on stage wasn't there as I knew I wasn't at my best. Backstage, I could see I wasn't outclassed, in fact it looked as if everybody else had just carried on their season the best they could, with no one looking outstanding in any way. Natural novice UK, 1996. Before long we were all lined up on stage.

As we went through the call outs, I felt little motivation, as I wasn't happy with what I was presenting, but fortunately I was the best of a bad bunch, so I took the title. I was where I wanted to be, with my biggest title yet, but it felt like a hollow victory. I knew then that it didn't matter whether my next competition was a local show or a world championship, whether there was one in the class or ten, what mattered was that next time I would fight to be at my best, and would be fired up, having done everything in my power to win.

I wrote this show off and never really mentioned it too much; the only thing good about that show was when Matt dropped his pants in front of the mirror, asking me if he was looking all right, when he wasn't even competing, with competitors that were, waiting to get a look, which even to this day I find funny. I would have left this show off the list altogether as it was one of my least favourites, it was the first time I hadn't enjoyed being on stage and even though I hate to admit it, this was the first time I questioned whether bodybuilding was for me. I didn't feel like a winner, so was just hoping the fire in my heart would reignite. My only strong point now was that I never quit, I always finished what I started, but still that wasn't going to be enough. I had accepted that genetically I wasn't really meant to succeed in my chosen sport for by now and with how hard I had worked I should have been much further up the ladder than where I was. To make it as a Mr Universe (world champion) I would have to pull out a few miracles, but at this point there was no magic in my mind or heart, only a lonely void of a reality that I didn't want to have to face. There were no young fan clubs anymore, and I could sense a lot of people had lost belief in me making it as a bodybuilder. Perhaps they could see that I had lost some belief myself.

With the shows now over, I was looking for a ray of light but initially couldn't see it. The gym was slowly but surely being neglected, Rob now ghost-like and distant, the upset of his career-destroying injury starting to show. Me and Lee had become like passing ships, with a lot of the old school guys slipping away one by one.

I started going out again, hoping for a bit of fun, and I had also been doing some door work, but I wasn't sure it was for me, or whether I wanted to give up all my weekends to do it. I started going out with a group of lads I had known a long time. At first it seemed good, and even when I was working the door we would all go out somewhere together afterwards. I thought this was what I needed, but it wasn't. Even the fun stuff like copping off had taken a different turn. It seemed like everyone was trying to get off with everyone else's girlfriends, and the girlfriends and wives of people I knew were knocking off with some of the lads I was hanging out with. I wasn't into cheating, I'm not saying I was perfect but I'd never played the stupid mind games that everyone seemed to be playing of late, so I knew it wouldn't be too long before these nights out came to an end.

I was told that a friend of ours had been hitting his girlfriend, but it wasn't until one night when I witnessed him bullying her that it really hit home. I didn't believe in hitting women so I couldn't let it rest. I grabbed the lad by his throat, forcing him back against a wall, then threatened him if he bullied her again. I knew his girlfriend quite well, which only made matters worse for him. As he backed away I could feel myself raging, but I knew it was more than this incident that had sent me this way. At this point in time I had a lot of raw anger that I was hoping would simmer, but I now had no friends I could trust, nor did I like or trust many women after what I had seen. My self-confidence was shot, with my sense of belonging not far behind. I couldn't fully understand my worsening anger and I wasn't the type of person who would want to talk about it either, but mostly I was doubting whether I had what it took to make it in bodybuilding, as I no longer had the focus I once possessed, I think that's where most of my frustration was coming from.

I started doing permanent weekends working the door. I didn't care much whether I lived or died, I felt that tightly sprung, I just needed to let loose, and with the club I worked at being 'fight

LIVING THE NIGHTMARE **BECOMING THE DREAM**

central' I had plenty to go at. Win or lose, I wasn't bothered. I would throw myself into fight after fight, sometimes hoping that someone would put me out of my misery, but after weeks of being banged, stamped on, kicked down steps, having to scrape myself up off the floor, I would still be in one piece and in most cases able to carry on. One night I had gotten into a fight with a group of lads, we were all going at each other, it was like being in a washing machine, everyone grabbing, punching, butting, biting – but all of a sudden there was no one there, and I realised I was the last man standing. I'm not quite sure how this happened but at this point I started to think that maybe it wasn't my time to check out just yet, so luckily I wouldn't have to die or do anything stupid; if anything it was working the doors that brought me round.

The group of lads I worked with became like brothers. There were a lot of big characters in the group, I was the quiet one, the rookie, but still I got stuck in all the same. A guy named Dozer, who ran the door, became a good friend and a positive influence in my life. Dozer would pick me up before work most weeks, and when asking him questions he would always have well thought-through answers. He was similar to Morpheus from The Matrix, but better looking! Before long I started asking him questions about life in general. He would sometimes laugh before answering, as the questions I asked could be quite random, just shit that was going on in my head mainly, but he put me right on a lot of things. His replies always came with a resolve, a straight yet fair answer, so over time my mind would ease up. Whilst working the door, Dozer had reinstalled me with self-belief, given me new sense of purpose, I was part of a team, I now had a place where I belonged and through this, had become more acceptant of the bigger world in which I lived.

I found that the bigger and stronger I became, the more powerful and effective I was on the doors, so for that reason my training picked up again. Matt was worried about me changing, and said that he didn't want me to get caught up with the doorman

lifestyle (women, dealing, gangsters, guns and messing with drugs).
I promised I wouldn't, and I never did.

I started boxing on Sundays, getting pretty good again, I learned
to use my power well and could soak up punishment like a sponge.
I did martial arts on Wednesdays, mainly Ninjitsu, but I learned some
fancy kicks too. I did weights Mondays, Tuesdays, Thursdays and
Fridays, martial arts on Wednesdays and boxing on Sundays. Once
again I lived to train, but it now had another purpose, being a good
doorman, having everyone's backs as they had mine.

I class this time in life as my growing up period, with certain
realities appearing not quite as they had seemed when I was young.
I found certain truths very tough to deal with, loyalties, true friends,
love, things I'd have gained easily when in my teens.

Over the past five or six years I had learnt more about life than I
ever did at school. I had spent twelve years in a classroom being told
how to be, what to study, what my next step in life should be. No one
ever actually tells you just how challenging, just how hard life really is.

I had tried to avoid getting involved with women, as my past
two short-term relationships hadn't worked out too well. I was
trying to steer clear of getting involved with anyone, but this would
prove to be harder than I first thought. One night while working
the doors I was approached by two girls; one was in my face and
very chatty, but the other just stood staring, looking to be weighing
me up. I was talking to the first girl but I couldn't keep my eyes off
the other, and it wasn't long before girl one got the message and
trotted off, leaving me to talk to her friend.

I first noticed this girl was amazingly attractive yet very innocent-
looking, she had the most beautiful blue eyes I'd ever seen. She was
talking away, and was very confident in how she spoke and sold
herself; I, on the other hand, had just been involved in a fight, and
had blood running down the side of my eye, still trying to tuck myself
in, sweat pouring from everywhere. I said I would meet her at the
end of the night as I didn't know what else to say, and I also wanted

to get cleaned up as I was feeling a bit uneasy about talking to her whilst in this state.

At the end of the night, she was sat downstairs waiting. I had planned loads of things I was going to say but ended up saying very little, luckily she gave me her number so I knew I could call her the next day. Her friend invited me back to the house but I said no as I was training the next morning. They both thought I was a bit strange. I gave her a quick peck on the lips, then quickly shot off like a bullet.

Her name was Christina and if she had been just your average girl I would have been able to be more myself, but this girl seemed right out of my league, so nerves had got the better of me. I phoned her twice the next day, but she wasn't in either time so I thought she wasn't interested, now trying my best not to think about her. The thought of this girl wouldn't go away, which in turn put me into a bad mood, I wished I had gone back with her the night before and got to know her. I was filled with anger and regret.

Later that night I got a call. On picking up the phone I heard a soft voice say, "Hello, is John there?" I instantly panicked, then felt myself going red, even though I was the only person in the house at the time. We started talking and before long had relaxed into a good conversation. There were no awkward silences and by the end of the chat we had got to know each other quite well, already arranging our first date. I felt a bit giddy that evening, a bit like a young teenager. It seemed odd – I had been taking life a little too seriously for some time now, and although still sceptical, I was now looking forward to the date, feeling like the cat that had got the cream.

Before going on the date I had to pick up some pointers from my friend Tom (as I had lost touch with my younger, cooler self). Tom was a renowned 'chick magnet', he got me set up with some new clothes, conversation tips and aftershaves. I even bought myself some new undies, as mine all had massive holes in the backsides looking like the moths had been at them. I was now set.

On turning up to the date, I saw Christina. She had turned up wearing a short black dress, looking nothing short of incredible, and had instantly reminded me of the Amanda Peterson character Cindy Mancini from the movie, Can't Buy Me Love, and also the movie, Fatal Charm, and just like those characters, she was the most loved and popular girl about town, talk about a dream come true.

The date went well, with things just starting to pick up. Later that year I rented a house next to my mum and dad; through my attitude, I'd not been close with my parents in a while so I thought it was time to make things good again. The end of the year made the start seem like a distant memory. With my new outlook on life I was looking forward to a good year with a new love, my old family and hopefully a successful bodybuilding season.

I HAD TRIED TO AVOID GETTING INVOLVED WITH WOMEN, AS MY PAST TWO SHORT-TERM RELATIONSHIPS HADN'T WORKED OUT TOO WELL.

It was this year that
I truly knew I loved her

CHAPTER 9

Love and positivity, the perfect year

In 1997, life had taken a big turn, an all-time high. By the spring we were all celebrating my dad's 50th birthday, we had become a family once more. On the same night I proposed to Christina, that one night was that rare moment in life when everything positive, everything good would come together.

The gym had taken on a new lease of life also. It had been taken over by a guy named Big Nick, who had formerly been a police officer. Rob and Lee were back training together, getting in shape for summer, they both seemed back to their old selves. Life on the door was better than ever and with my self-destruct button now switched off, the anger of the previous year had become this year's confidence.

It was a magnificent sunny year, and even though I had been with Christina just over ten months, it was this year that I truly knew I loved her. We would spend hours talking on the phone throughout the week, but the times when she came and stopped with me at the weekends, that was priceless. Most weekends after working the club, when Christina came back to mine, I would bring down the old mattress from upstairs, laying it out in front of the open fire, kissing and cuddling, barely sleeping, wrapped up in blankets, watching the sun come up, still awake from the night before. We would share long walks on sunny days, saying words we meant, and would be excited about every day, every conversation, every kiss. It felt like how it looked in the movies, a love I had yearned for, a time I would cherish, never to be forgotten.

There was a close community feel around where we lived, with most of the neighbours being chatty and easy going. The kids on the street were cheeky yet funny, and I would sometimes catch them climbing up our drainpipe trying to see Christina getting changed! I used to teach the kids on the street how to skate, with a lot of the door lads regularly popping round, with us all hanging out at mine, my sister Karen often getting chatted up when they were about. I couldn't have been any happier, I enjoyed getting back to being the person I once was, it had been a while. So now with positivity at its highest it was time to see if I could add it to the up-coming contest season.

I had devised a very different diet to what I had in prior years. I would start Monday, Tuesday with moderate-low calories, then Wednesday I would add higher carbs and fats, then Thursday, Friday and Saturday I would completely bottom-out, with very low calories and virtually zero carbs come Saturday. Sunday I would treat myself to what I wanted from 12 till 4pm in the afternoon. This plan came as I now knew my body would only burn fat when on very low carbs, but also knew that it would eventually shut down, so that's why I added the Wednesday spike and the Sunday treat day.

I was thinking on my feet, finally starting to understand what worked for me. I knew there was a large scientific element to bodybuilding, but that there was also a common sense aspect to it also. My own body would work differently to others, you yourself were a science, and a science you would have to know well in order to progress. I had enjoyed coming into shape this year, and had now started to be seen as an up-comer with potential to do well.

I was well received by Nick, the new owner of the gym, and had become good friends with both him and Cyril the manager. Christina also enjoyed being part of gym life, coming with me quite often throughout the week. I regularly saw Big Lee in the cardio room with us sometimes talking about times gone by. Lee would always regret not going to the Mr Universe, he would say to me, "If you ever get the chance to go, don't do what I did and just presume there will be a next time."

Lee was quite lucky as he was also intelligent, he had shifted his passion for bodybuilding, using it to start working his way up the management ladder at work. Eventually he became very successful. I didn't really have that option, I was no quiz kid when it came to anything outside of my chosen sport, so I kept Lee's words with me, as I never wanted to be faced with that type of regret. I wasn't sure if I could move on from it as well as he had.

I was the only person to compete out of Silver's during 1997 so more people than usual took an interest. I enjoyed the attention which was coming my way, as I had always shied away from it when I'd competed in the past. The likes of Rob, Matt and Lee were also commenting on my improvement.

My confidence had grown so much, I now wanted to give a demo of the routine I had put together for some of the gym members and staff, to see what they thought. As I went into the posing room Cyril asked what I was posing to, and I said "East 17, 'House of Love'"; he laughed, as did a few of the others, but I knew how good the routine was so I didn't take them on, I just turned on the music and started. I could see their faces as I started to pose; they were smiling, looking at each other, looking at me, then nodding. They thought the routine was very good and the track was fitting. I knew it would go down well; although other aspects of my bodybuilding were suffering, I knew my posing to be top notch.

I'd taught myself to pose through watching video after video of the best routines, with most of the guys whose routines I liked having studied ballet in order to get the flow and posture right. Roger Shelley, the photographer, was also an important influence, moving various poses, making them better, much more graceful, I would learn a lot from him. I would choreograph around five or six routines a year in my off-season, so they were already well rehearsed and without fault when contest time came. All I would have to do then was pick out my favourite.

Contest time was now here, and I had decided to do the Mr England show as my main event. The show was run by a guy named Lee Kemp who had done quite well as a junior but was now an official for a European bodybuilding federation, while running this show as his own. It felt more welcoming here than a lot of the shows I had done in the past, and as I was at my best, this all just added to the excitement.

The guys in the line-up were all of a good standard, in the past I couldn't have competed with them, but this time was different. I took second place but wasn't outclassed even by the guy who had won, receiving good feedback on how I looked. Even though I didn't take the title I had looked my best to date and had enjoyed the whole experience. It felt a lot better to lose being at my best than to win some half-arsed contest where I was just the best of a bad bunch. This year had turned out to be one of the best years of my life, I knew that the positivity I had brought into it had somehow helped in how I looked, thought and felt. I hoped this feeling would last, so was now looking forward to the year ahead with great optimism.

Unfortunately, my form at work wasn't as good as my form in the gym.

The New Year started with a bang. I was training with Dozer, Lomax and Ivan, all door lads at the place I worked at, we were hitting it hard with me now beating a lot of my personal bests. I felt I was gaining a good amount of muscle, with my form also at its best so there was very little chance of injury. Unfortunately though, my form at work wasn't as good as my form in the gym.

I had worked on the mail for some years, but on this one particular round there were no drop-off points for the first couple of miles, leaving me to carry a heavy bag a lot further than I should have had to. I complained to the manager as my neck would become increasingly tight, but I would get the response of "Don't be soft, I thought you were a weight lifter?"

As the weeks went on I became progressively weaker, and didn't know why; I didn't know much about trapped nerves at this time. Finally I came into work not even able to lift my arms, so I had to go home on sick. I went to see a doctor who first told me about the trapped nerves; initially I didn't think it was too bad, until he told me it would take up to six months to put right and that I would have to shed a lot of my muscle in order to be treated properly. As if that wasn't enough, he told me I might not be able to train again.

I felt quite ill, realising I hadn't even been on the British stage, let alone won the title. I also became worried about whether Christina would still want to be with me if I lost weight and wasn't a doorman any more. She had always loved the life, so I wasn't sure how she would be if it was just us two. Mostly I feared becoming nothing, not being able to fulfil my dreams of building the perfect body the way I had hoped.

I started my assault on the weight loss by wearing a shrunk down tracksuit top so I could use the pockets to put my hands in, this would take the pressure from my shoulders. I started going out on short walks in the morning, and changed my diet so that I was eating a lot less. I wanted to get the weight off as quickly so I could be treated as soon as possible, then hopefully get back into the gym. After a couple of weeks I had got used to this way of life, at least I had an aim. It turned out Christina really did love me and she would come up even more now I had to be looked after, she actually enjoyed spending the extra time with me.

The guys from the gym were always in touch and kept telling me to pop by for a brew so, as I had not seen any of them for a while, I decided to go down. When I first walked in the gym I was instantly welcomed by Nick and Cyril, then Nick made us all a coffee as we sat down to talk. I noticed he had put a window from the foyer into the gym, so you could see everyone training, it was a good idea but as I peered through I suddenly felt overwhelmingly sick. Everyone in there was looking good, all training hard; I could sense the hunger in the atmosphere. Nick's voice seemed to fade away as I retreated into my own little world; my thoughts ran on, "What if I can never do this again?" Panicked and upset, I gulped the hot black coffee, burning the top of my mouth, made my excuses for leaving, then left. I thought I was going to burst if I stayed, and knew I wouldn't be going back there again unless it was to train.

From this point on I focussed on my everyday routine, starting with a walk in the hills followed by a sleep. I would look forward to seeing Christina, and enjoyed it when she came to see me. It was the night times that were the problem, but even that would soon be sorted. I would go to see my mate Z in the evening; he was into video games, so before long I was playing FIFA 98 and became obsessed with the game 'Goldeneye', which I would play every night until gone midnight, trying to complete it. With all this in place I could keep my mind off training for a while.

In a short time my walk had become a run, with my hands now starting to free up a little after a series of osteopath and acupuncture sessions; I was also starting to get stronger. I enjoyed my morning runs in the hills, knowing my fitness was returning. When I initially went back to work I was placed on sorting, and happily I found myself working next to Rob, who was also now working as a mail man. I told Rob what the doctor had said about me not being able to train again. He just looked at me then replied, "John, you've been training for over seven years now, all your body knows is how to recover. If it was anyone else then yes, but you're not just anyone else." And just like that, Rob had got my head back in the game. I was just hoping my body would soon follow.

Rob's words had been like gold to me, almost instantly putting the doctor's opinion on the back burner; it was just what I had needed to hear, and not long afterwards I was back in the gym. I had been training around six or seven weeks but nothing seemed to be happening, then one day out of the blue I got an almighty pump, my arms looked enormous! It was probably because the rest of me looked so thin, but still I knew at this point that I was back. On that same evening Rob came up just as I had finished my work out, wanting me to have a look at him. He had told me he was competing but asked me to keep it quiet until he was certain. As he stripped down I remembered the reason why I had got into bodybuilding in the first place, his physique was inch perfect, every muscle group complimenting the next, peaks then separation running through every muscle and with a tiny waist to boot. I'd forgotten how good he was. Rob was back, bringing a flagship of motivation with him, and now back to my old fitness, I was ready to get on board.

PANICKED AND UPSET, I GULPED THE HOT BLACK COFFEE, MADE MY EXCUSES FOR LEAVING, THEN LEFT. I THOUGHT I WAS GOING TO BURST IF I STAYED.

Christina was always airing
the house out...

CHAPTER 10

Setting up house

Later that same year I faced another challenge, as Christina and I decided to buy a house and move in together. This would be the first time I had lived with a woman, so right away there would be difficulties. Before moving in I had told Christina that I ate six meals a day, trained all week and had no plans on changing any of this in the near future. With her acceptance of this I thought there would be no problem, but from the get go even the meal times had her thrown. Christina would ask me what time tea was, presuming it was around the 5.30pm mark, I told her I ate at 4pm so that I was finished for 4.30pm and had a full hour and half to digest my food before training, and that I ate again around 7.30pm; so she had the choice of two tea times.

Christina didn't quite understand at first, I could see that for a normal person it would seem odd, but after a month or two of acclimatising it became the norm. She struggled with the smell of eggs, and was always airing the house out. She would also look embarrassed when purchasing 200 eggs a week at the supermarket! When the girls behind the check-out desks asked whether we were caterers or making a big cake, she would just bow her head, or go a little red, leaving her even more embarrassed. But over a couple of months Christina had learned to live with a bodybuilder, and would be eating and training like one too.

I was continuing to keep in touch with Matt. After his success on stage he had been picked up by well-known nutritionists and gurus in his bid for pro-stardom, but things didn't seem to be going as well as I had hoped for my young up-coming friend. Matt's personality had started to change, with his sense of humour compromised, he had become edgy and would have frequent aggressive outbursts. He had competed this year but his usual picture-perfect physique had looked bloated, and he didn't seem to be of sound mind when speaking to him. I was worried, but at this time I had little influence. He had drifted into a new crowd so I just hoped he would be OK. I was always there if he needed me, this he knew. For now I didn't delve too much as I didn't know all the ins and outs, and had my own work cut out coming back after injury.

1999, 25 years of age. I knew I had to work harder than ever, in order to come back better than ever. I had been on the mend now for around three months, but was at that stage where I was starting to feel super-human. Because of the time off I'd had, I was fully rested, ready to fire up once more. I had my game plan all set. First I wanted to break the 15 stone barrier, then I wanted to get up to the 60kg dumbbells our gym had just brought in, as well as beat all my personal bests. After this I would diet back down, get shredded, then finally get to the Britain, hopefully being good enough to make the night show where only the final five or six were placed. The previous year hadn't been progressive, so now I would have to make sure I was up to where I would have been if I hadn't had my setback. I only had limited time, but I wouldn't use the past year as an excuse; there would be no excuse for failure.

Z and Renny were my off-season training partners as they were both massively keen, strong and good spotters, so it was time to go to war. The year progressed as I had hoped, in fact it went even better as now I wasn't just known for my physique, I was also known for my strength, with a lot of people saying pound-for-pound I was one of the strongest guys in the gym. At my best during this year I was pressing the 60kg dumbbells for fun, dead lifting 230kg, but my finest hour came as my once weak squat was now up to 250kg, out-powering most of the others. I had also reached my 15-stone benchmark, so I had surpassed every goal I had set myself; this very rarely happens but on this occasion God had been kind.

NOW I WASN'T JUST KNOWN FOR MY PHYSIQUE, I WAS ALSO KNOWN FOR MY STRENGTH, WITH A LOT OF PEOPLE SAYING POUND-FOR-POUND I WAS ONE OF THE STRONGEST GUYS IN THE GYM

CHAPTER 11

Rob Worthington The man, the myth, the legend

It was coming close to contest preparation time, 1999, and I knew I would only be able to train with one partner as the work rate increases the closer you get to a contest. Rob and I had become close over the past year, and we were both planning to compete, so we decided to become a team, training together up to the shows. It didn't take long until we were in full flow, with every new workout better than the last. We fed off one another's energy, which just added to the workouts. There was no competitive rivalry, we both just really wanted to see the other do well; it was perfect. Silver's had become very popular, with a string of new members ranging from young lads starting out to lads-about-town, old members returning, and new faces we didn't know. The gym had never been more alive. Christina was my cardio partner and was loving the gym life, she had taken on a strict diet, so life at home was also much easier.

My diet for this year was porridge, egg-whites in the morning then again after training, followed by turkey and broccoli the rest of the day, with two portions of broccoli being cooked and two being uncooked. My reason for this combination was that cooked broccoli allows you to digest more needed nutrients, whilst the uncooked broccoli takes more calories to digest than it contains, as it is very high in fibre. It also helps rid your body of water retention whilst keeping hunger at bay, and with the added bonus of having large amounts of vitamins A and C it was also good for fighting off unwanted viruses. Broccoli was a superfood that was going to get me super ripped.

Christina and I had just bought a house but Christina was still only a trainee where she worked so, to make life easier, I did a couple more half-rounds in the week, on overtime. I would power-walk whilst on the rounds, treating it as an aerobic workout. I always made sure that at least one of my sessions was on leg day, as after leg training I was finished. I thought it a good idea to do the day's aerobics earlier – and I was getting paid for it as well. In years gone by, when dieting I had always avoided being around the smell of nice food, because of the temptation, but now a stronger person it was different. I would finish work, but before I caught the bus home I would take what became my ritual route around Bury, going past all the lovely-smelling eateries, just standing there sniffing up the scent of all the freshly cooked food. I think I did this most days as for some reason it brought me a strange pleasure, but it would bring even stranger looks from passers-by! If I was ever at my mum's when they ordered pizza, they thought it the norm for me to want to sniff the pizza boxes before they ate, and would always laugh about it.

Christina had also come to be in good shape, to the point where I once walked into the gym just noticing these ripped peaked arms; it wasn't until I heard her ask what I was looking at that I looked up and realised it was her! If I hadn't known her, she could have quite easily passed herself off as a top fitness model.

Me and Rob had been training a while now, and had got ourselves in good shape, so it was time to have a look at ourselves in the main mirror that was in the gym. By the time I had undone my training boots and taken off my shirt, I stood up to find virtually everybody in the gym standing behind me, wanting to see what I looked like. There had always been one or two, but on this day there must have been nearly 30 people stood watching. I initially felt overwhelmed, but had to just carry on by hitting a few poses. The crowd clapped and even cheered as I went from pose to pose. It was a massive buzz, I now realised how I was seen in the eyes of others. I had finally become a person that other people wanted to be.

Rob was already used to this kind of reception but even he looked a little stunned by the crowd and the reaction we got. We were the rock stars of our gym world! Every night I would now look forward to being in the gym. The feeling I got when in there was electric. Every machine we went near, people would just move or go on something else; every time we went near a mirror, or just lifted our arms, or our shirts, to take a glimpse, someone would always be looking over. People were just randomly telling us we were looking good, sometimes just standing watching us train.

> *People were just randomly telling us we were looking good, sometimes just standing watching us train.*

I had waited for this a long time and was loving every minute. It got to the point where Rob and I would just be expecting people to move out of our way, so it came as a shock when one day, whilst we were both stood looking at ourselves in the mirror, a woman just came up and jumped on the machine in front of us, blocking our view. Reality bit for a few seconds, with us both stepping back looking at each other, then Rob just said, "We're not as important as we think we are, are we?" I've got to say this really made me giggle.

Despite this being a great year it was still very tough. I had dieted and trained to my limits, but could never feel sorry for myself as I knew Rob was going through the same. In fact, he was going through much worse. Over the period of 12 weeks going up to the contest Rob would suffer four major injuries, with two of them ending with him on the operating table. Early on in his prep he had to go into hospital for a hernia operation. Normal recovery time, five weeks, Rob was back in the gym within two. He then tore a muscle at the top of his thigh, followed by finding out he was suffering with scoliosis coming from his lower back, but none of this slowed him down. You could see the pain in his face, and sometimes in his movement, but not once would he complain or make any excuse not to be in the gym.

But the next injury would be a tester even for Rob. Once more he tore his pec, and had to go back into hospital to have it reattached. Training together after this had to change. We would still turn up together but would separate, as Rob had to work around his injuries on certain movements, but would still be giving his all. I had seen Rob just after he had suffered his initial pec tear four years earlier, he had looked like a broken man, but now, even with all the added injury, he had become a man on fire. Rob had once reminded me of The Terminator, but now I knew he really was one! Nothing would stop him this year, and even not knowing the outcome of how he would look or place didn't seem to faze him. It was like Rocky II when Apollo Creed's trainer says to Apollo, "I saw you beat that man harder than any man I've ever seen beat before, but the man just kept coming back." That was Rob, he was like Terminator, Rocky and Westworld all rolled into one, he was Mad Max, Road Warrior, and he wasn't going to stop for anyone.

> *That was Rob, he was like Terminator, Rocky and Westworld all rolled into one, he was Mad Max, Road Warrior, and he wasn't going to stop for anyone.*

Rob went on to have a good season that year, placing third in the under-90kg British Final, whilst still in recovery. Back at his best, he went on to win the Class 3 British, as well as the overall. This would be Rob's last major year of competition, as he pursued his next step in life. By spring 2000 he was training pro-wrestlers and

American footballers over in the USA. Rob had an amazing career, winning a string of British titles, as well as being Mr Universe, and a former Strong Man champion. He appeared as a guest on Top Gear, was featured in magazines and had small roles in movies, but it was in 1999 when he earned the undying respect of anyone who was around the gym at that time. His impressive contest record was nothing compared to his desire to win. I would always be thankful for what I had witnessed and learned from this very strong yet humble character.

My season would soon be starting, I felt set for the Britain, but first I would have to qualify. Cyril and I were doing the same show; Rob had already qualified through being a former champion. I had seen Cyril a lot over this year, with us becoming good friends; he was a big character but would be quite private when it came to people having a look at him, only showing the chosen few. He was a massive man and was competing at the 18-19 stone mark if I remember correctly. He was a good guy, but didn't suffer fools.

We would often talk about the Britain as none of us had ever been there. When we chose the shows we were going to do, we decided we would travel up together, including the ladies in our lives and some of our friends. Luckily our first show was only a 20 minute drive away. When we got to the venue I noticed there were six or seven rows of seats all reserved for Silver's Gym. Unknown to me, Nick the gym owner had been sorting out the fan base, it had got to the point where he had to book a full section of the theatre. This was flattering, I knew there would be a roar of applause for us when we appeared on stage.

I was now at an Intermediate level in bodybuilding, and for those who don't know what this means, if you win a national championship at Junior or Novice level you then step up to Intermediate, then if you finish in the final five in the night show at the British Championship you would have to step up again to become a 'Mr'. This class is the most competitive and prestigious in the bodybuilding arena, it was my aim to get there in the coming year. Just to carry on with this: if you're lucky enough to become British champion you may get selected to go for the Mr Universe title (world championship) depending on the Federation, then once you start placing in the top five, top six, even sometimes top ten, you're likely to start getting invites for the big international world championships. If you keep turning up in shape and placing in the top five, top six bracket, this is when you are world class, with most of these shows being top level amateur, pro-am or of a professional level. When you're the best of the best at a world standard then usually steps are made to make it to the Mr Olympia, the ultimate contest of them all.

My line up was called out, there were nine of us on stage. The whole Intermediate line up was to be judged at once, even though there were two weight classes, over and under 80kg. I was in the under 80s, only one from this class would go through to the final, unless I could get into the overall top three, as all the top three went through on this day. The call outs I received were good, I felt very competitive. I was clearly at my best, now competing at a different level. I could hear the applause and shouts from the crowd. It was going to be close between me and another lad, I felt we were both fighting for the third spot overall and for the first spot in the 80kg bracket, so it looked like all or nothing.

I loved being out on stage, with the close competition getting me and the crowd massively revved up. Once more the stage felt like home, with a good following similar to when I had won the Mr Bury many moons ago. When we went off stage I was greeted by Cyril, who was saying everyone thought I would make the top three, and that I would also win the under 80kg bracket, so I was feeling stoked, ready set to blast back out on stage for the final results.

Only the top five were called back out with both me and my rival in there, standing in line, patiently waiting for the verdict. The names came in, and in fifth was my rival, leaving me elated – now I would be the winner of the under 80kg bracket, which would take me through to the British finals. I wondered who would be fourth... and then I found out – it was me. I was slightly shocked, the guy who had come in third wasn't even in our league, with the crowd being first to let him know, booing and shouting abuse at the judges. I was slightly peeved but knew that I was going to the British anyway now, and would only be against my own weight for when it came.

When I had left the stage, I got changed then went straight to the front desk to get my invite. I told the official that it hadn't been awarded on stage and asked him to find it for me. The official soon came back, only to tell me that I hadn't qualified, because the guy who had won the whole class was also under 80kg! The guy had looked massive, I couldn't believe what had just happened. I went back to my seat and found Big Lee. He had spoken to one of the judges who had said that my tan had looked bad, and that

> *My tan had looked bad, otherwise I would have definitely been in the top three*

otherwise I would have definitely been in the top three, which would have also got me through to the British final. With this news I broke down. I had my hands on my head as my feelings of being so close to Heaven had gone diving straight back down to Hell.

As we left the building I saw Cyril. I was ranting, saying I was going to eat loads of pizza and that the show had been a fix. After a short while of listening to me go on, Cyril's face suddenly turned serious, he grabbed me by my tracksuit till we were face to face, and said, "You're not having anything to eat, there's a qualifier next week, you're going to be there; I'm going to pick you up and you better be ready!" And with that, my thoughts of eating pizza and giving up were all now answered, without me even having to make a decision.

The week soon went by, and like clockwork Cyril was at my door. As he came in he said, "Let's have a look." We went upstairs. As I stripped down in front of the mirror, Cyril just glared, then nodded and in his usual manner said, "Good laaad", then said I was looking better than I had the week before. Then he dropped his own pants to show off his legs – in all fairness, they wouldn't have looked out of place on a rhino.

At the show this time there was no fan club, only me, Cyril, Rob and the girls, as well as a handful of friends. But today wasn't about the turn out, it was about the result. This was the last qualifier, and the toughest show to qualify at, so the nerves were now playing up and the call to get on stage couldn't come soon enough. The stage would be full when walking on, and had to be divided into two lines in order to be properly viewed. I think there were around eight in my class, and even more in the heavier section, but this time we would only be judged in our own weight, which meant there was only one spot up for grabs.

Former World Champion Charlie Claremont was just roaming around the place, and all the TV Gladiators were drinking at the bar.

I knew I was in the running as I seemed to be in every call out, but I knew it was close for that very same reason; and obviously close wasn't going to be good enough. We were all brought back out with the line-up spanning the full length of the stage as we waited to hear the result. "And the winner of the under 80kg section goes to John McLoughlin. John, could you please collect your invitation for the British finals before you leave?" Job done. I was over the moon, now looking forward to the congratulations, and to a bag of goodies Christina and I had picked out to eat after the show.

When we got back to our seats everyone congratulated me, but they were laughing at the same time, then looking at Christina. She had been unable to resist the food and the bag was now full of empty wrappers, she hadn't left me a scrap. She looked up at me, her cheeks bulging with the last of the flapjack, trying not to laugh.

I couldn't stay mad for long, but I dare say if I hadn't won it would probably have been a different story. It had been a good day with Cyril also qualifying, it was now time to get back and prepare for what would be the first British final for us both.

Two weeks went by quickly. I never once veered from the diet, punishing myself more than ever. Unlike last time I had competed, I would only have a treat once every two to three weeks, and if for any reason the treat meal would rest heavy, I would put my fingers down my throat and throw the food back up, as I couldn't bear the thought of wasting time having to burn it off again. I knew this wasn't right so I decided that in the last month, I wouldn't treat at all. I found the broccoli was a winner as I never hit a wall, I carried on burning fat right until the end, never flattening out once. The diet and the hard work took me to where I wanted to be, the British final.

On entering the venue I quickly realised that anyone who was anyone was there. Former World Champion Charlie Claremont was just roaming around the place, and all the TV Gladiators were drinking at the bar. The thought of competing in front of all these well-known people was another thing altogether. On this year Silver's had four people competing at the Britain – me, Cyril, Rob and a girl called Heather. Heather didn't bother much with the rest of us. She had adopted a professional attitude towards the sport and was walking around like a billboard, with sponsors' logos on everything she wore, with barely any recognition for the rest of us. We left her to it, but being the guys we were, we were polite anyway.

The day had been long drawn out, but at last it was my turn to compete. As soon as I got onto the stage the nerves were kicking in, there wasn't a single person in the line-up who hadn't turned up in their best shape. I felt nervous until I got my first call out, but from then onwards it was all systems go. I seemed to be in the firing line from that point on. I was taking centre stage in a lot of call outs, and was even called out with the two guys I had down to win it. I felt I was up there with the best of them, even when competing at such a good level, so when coming off stage I was hoping to be short-listed for the final placings.

I came off stage. The people in the Silver's camp were saying third, maybe fourth, with the odd one saying fourth, maybe fifth. At this moment I was just waiting to be short-listed for the night show. When the list was put up, I was on there. I was relieved, as now I had hit my goal, I just had to see if I could step it up once more, hopefully making it into the top three.

By the night show I was more relaxed and I felt more pumped when going back on in the evening. There was a superb atmosphere as we posed down before the final placings. When the placings were announced it wasn't long before I heard my name called. I knew it was close, as I had beaten the guy who had come in third only a few weeks before, but I also realised it was just one of those things and that everyone had to be placed somewhere. I had reached my goal of getting into the final five (or final six, whichever the cut-off point was), and knew I was as good as anyone up to the final three. The top two guys were in a league of their own, so there had never been any possibility of winning, but being at my best I had no regrets.

It was a good end to a great competitive season. On that evening Rob had placed third, and Cyril sixth or seventh, I'm not too sure. I'm also not sure where Heather placed, but I know she was eating Jelly Tots and drinking beer after the morning show, her ego and professionalism nowhere to be seen. I'm glad to say that after this experience she reverted back to being the nice girl she once was, and I think she finally realised that there was more to being a bodybuilder than just wearing fancy logos. This was the last time she ever competed.

1999 was now at a close. I'd had a great year in bodybuilding, and had also proved my worth on the door more than ever. My relationship with Christina had come a long way, we had become closer than ever. I realised that she had been there for me, doing the things I liked, sharing in my dreams, moving to my town, it was now time for me to do the one thing she wanted most. It was time to plan our wedding, giving Christina her well-deserved time in the spotlight.

At the end of the decade, I realised just how many bodybuilders had been and gone. Every one of them once carrying the dream I had. I had seen every scenario, from drug addiction, body shut-down, depression, women, lives of crime and just plain bad luck destroy so many people's lives and careers, with most of them never getting past Junior or Novice level. I'd seen, and I'd learnt from it, but without having to pay any dividend myself. I had surpassed most of what these guys had done, so was now very appreciative of my position. On a more positive note I had also witnessed guys I had trained with making it, with my friend John Hodgson winning his pro card on this year. Come 2001 I would be in the big league. I knew there was going be no let-up – if anything I would have to work even harder.

COME 2001 I WOULD BE IN THE BIG LEAGUE I KNEW THERE WAS GOING BE NO LET-UP IF ANYTHING I WOULD HAVE TO WORK EVEN HARDER.

I had just had the best
day of my life

CHAPTER 12

Wedding bells and bliss

As we moved into the new millennium, life was again on the up, with my popularity now at a new height. Around the gym I would be constantly attentive, as helpful as I had promised I would be many years earlier. Writing diets, showing people how to bring up weak points, using intensity, being positive minded, these were just a few of my uses around the gym. My own training was also at an all-time high. I had mentioned to Nick about getting some bigger dumbbells, so when the 75kgs turned up, I had to take the bull by the horns and get using them. I felt bad at times as there was only me and Nick who could actually lift them at all, but Nick didn't seem to bother, and it was a good personal best for me. By now I was using the 50kg dumbbells on shoulder press, I was dead-lifting 250kg, bent over row 190kg and averaging an off-season weight of around 15 stone plus.

I had been headhunted by a rep from a large nutrition company that had turned me down twice before. This time when the rep had showed the company owner my photos he had been more than impressed, so had wanted to see me. I was invited along to be viewed, and interviewed for sponsorship. The rep was a little guy named Allan Tyrer who had also worked on the post; he had looked out for me a long time, so when I got the call back for the interview he had been more than excited for me.

My life on the door had been hectic, if not a touch dangerous, but by early summer of this year the danger had subsided with me back on easy street. I had an entourage of young wannabe bodybuilding bouncers at my beck and call, as well as great sets of friends from my day job and at the gym. Christina and I were getting on well, keeping busy with our wedding planning. So, in other words, things couldn't have been much better for me at this time.

When the interview for my sponsorship came around I was excited, the thought of this side of bodybuilding where I would be seen and promoted was very much for me. I had already built up a professional reputation around the gym so thought this to be the next step up. As I entered the building I noticed it was a lot smarter than I had expected, my name was listed in gold letters on the notice board, and I was spoken to very courteously as I waited for the interview. I was called in, then greeted by an elderly gentleman by the name of Arthur. He was an old timer who had at some point in his career competed against the great Arnold Schwarzenegger, so was soon telling stories of a seemingly better age of bodybuilding that he had been a part of.

I had enjoyed the interview, thinking things were going well, but when at the end of the interview he asked me to strip down I couldn't do it! I realised I had only let anyone see me when I was pumped and in great shape. Even when I was in the gym and looking pretty good I would never entertain even wearing a vest. Arthur was trying to convince me, saying that I would have to go to shows and wear vests at the sales-stands. Even during my off-season I would have to look good enough to take part in photo-shoots for his magazine. I still wasn't for stripping down, but I said he could use my photos, and when contest time came I would be glad to do training photos. I had started to feel a little uneasy for some reason, so was ready to leave, I didn't think I had sealed the deal.

On the way out Arthur shook my hand saying he had decided to give me the sponsorship, and that he was looking forward to working with me when I was ready. I was really surprised! But very happy. I would represent Arthur's company for many years, and at the end it would be me who would call it a day. I always promoted Arthur's products, but never once would I attend any type of convention, or be part of any off-season photo shoots. Through this experience I realised I was quite introverted in a certain way, as I would only ever show myself when I felt ready. The bit of money and exposure I would get from the sponsorship wasn't worth my dignity, being seen how I wanted to be seen would always be the most important thing for me. I did strip down close to, or just after, contests for Arthur, but I was glad it was when I was ready, as he would gather all his staff around to have a look whenever I was there. I didn't mind as long as I was looking the way I wanted to look. Both Allan and Arthur said I was like a young Samir Bannout. I was always thankful to Allan; he was one of the few people who had believed in me from the start.

Life in the gym was good, I was back in training with Z and Renny, and now an old-timer by the name of Mark who had once mentored me was also back. Mark had helped me in years gone by, but over the years I would know him more through socialising than through competitive bodybuilding. He had been working for his degree in law since I'd known him, and had recently graduated with honours so was now making a good living working as a solicitor. He had noted and even pointed out that I had built up a good reputation throughout the gym, he seemed surprised with the progress I had made in both strength and muscle gain. Now he was talking about his own come-back in the year to come.

I could sense in how he spoke that he wanted to get his bodybuilding reputation back to what it once was. I think he just presumed that he would return to become respected. He hadn't thought that five years of drinking, bad eating, fighting and womanising might get in his way; why should it? He had never failed in anything he had set his mind on so far. This was only a passing thought for me at that time; he was being more than supportive in preparation for my wedding at this time.

I had organised all my groomsmen, starting with Mark, Barny, Z and Renny; in other words, my current training partners. Z seemed a little put out, he thought he was going to be the Best Man as I had spent a lot of time with him, but my logic was to go for my longest serving friend, someone outside of the gym circle.

I decided to go with my old friend Simon Jaworski, as he had always kept in touch no matter where life had taken him, and had been a good friend for way longer than any other. The lead up to the wedding was a blast, with 50 or 60 people turning up to my stag do, to wish me the best. We went paint-balling in the afternoon, myself and my mate Jay Barnes got blasted at Gross Point Blank, as I was the groom and he was being gobby so had to take the place of the Best Man, so had to run with me. Despite the big turnout on the day, it was only me and my mate Ernie who would survive to the end of the night, and I only have a vague memory of karate chopping poppadums in some curry house then looking for Ernie in the taxi line with him laid on his back, only able to see the bottom of his shoes, funny. It was a great send off.

The next week soon arrived, bringing my wedding. I woke early and for some reason felt the need to go to the gym first thing. I saw Nick as he came into the gym wondering if he had got the day right, he was laughing when I told him he had. Back at home the crowds were gathering, with my mum doing her best to make everyone a cup of tea. I was raring to go with the day so far already being a blast. The church ceremony went well, apart from the priest not knowing any of our names and Simon having to keep correcting him, which I found funny. Both myself and Christina were giggling nervously whilst trying to say our vows. I took her to be my wife so was now the happiest man on the planet.

My speech sounded like something Rocky would say, as I never realised I had to make one, so I just kept it short and sincere. Simon's speech was well rehearsed, with me just being ripped to bits without a single good word said, leaving everyone in stitches. As the speeches were finished Barny filled his mouth with helium from one of the balloons, raised a glass, then yelled out "To the bride and groom" in a squeaky voice, leaving everyone clapping and laughing.

At the evening event the place was packed, everyone in good spirits, feeding off the lively atmosphere. Even Barny shed a few tears, telling me how highly he thought of me, telling me what a good person I was. I was quite taken aback, this would be the first and last time I would see him this way. By the end of the night I realised I had just had the best day of my life witnessing total happiness, even then I didn't think it possible I would ever feel this happy again. The day after our wedding we set off for our two-week honeymoon.

It had turned out to be a great and very memorable year, with my last competitive year at an all-time high; now this year enjoying wedding bliss as well as getting my first major sponsorship. I was now more positive than ever so was looking forward to the coming year.

2001 hit, I already had my battle plan. I was selecting which shows I was going to do as well as planning my diets up to the selected dates, but it would be months before I needed to diet down and there was something I needed to do first. I had spoken to Lee and Rob about six or seven years previously, Lee had asked me how big I wanted to be, I said I wanted to be as big as Rob. Lee told me that off season Rob was 16 stone, he then asked if I ever thought I would get to that, my reply being "Yes".

I was currently 15 and a half stone so I thought my goal before dieting would be to hit this target. After having to eat excessively for a few months I finally got there. I looked as big as a house. The aim wasn't about whether it was all muscle, it was mainly about sticking to my word, doing what I said I would, and that anything is possible if you're willing to keep working at it. The fact that I couldn't bend down to tie my shoe laces, and was going to have get down to the under-80kg class later in the year, didn't matter.

This was now a battle of wits,
as well as weights

CHAPTER 13

The rivalry

The first half of the year would see me getting as big and strong as possible while getting behind a couple of my old friends who were both looking to make their come-back in bodybuilding. Matt was the most noted, he hadn't competed for three years through numerous reasons, but for the past 12 months had got himself looking better than ever, to the point you wouldn't have thought he had ever been away. After training together one day we both decided to have a look. I looked massive in clothes, but was pretty fat, as you would expect off season, I was around sixteen stone four at this point. Matt looked a bit fat with his clothes on, but when he had stripped down he looked shredded and massive, weighing in at 18-plus. With him looking nothing short of a top five Olympian, he looked to have it made. Mark (a former mentor and a British champion in the mid-1980s), on the other hand, had been living the student lifestyle, but he too had now settled down, and had put in a good year. He had already made himself a realistic five-year plan to win a British title.

Mark had become a well-known business man, but was now forgotten in the bodybuilding world, as he had not competed for around 11-12 years. He was trying to get himself back on the map. I wanted to be there for them both, spotting, putting them right on how they looked, right up to going to the shows, helping backstage, the whole thing. It was what I had always done. I was looking forward to seeing them both, but unfortunately there was only one who would make it back.

I had been waiting for Matt to go training, he said he would be late but wanted my opinion on something. When he arrived he had his arm in a sling, he told me how he had suffered a pec tear. His whole chest was black, but it didn't look misshapen. I felt bad for him, but truly thought he would be OK, so just told him everything he needed to hear to put his mind at ease. Matt was thankful for my words, he had offered his help and advice for when I needed it.

It was Mark that was ready to make the come-back, he seemed back to his old self, back doing the sport he loved the most. I had kept an eye on his progress, with us starting to grab a few workouts together in the week. Mark was his own man, he had already been mingling with well-known bodybuilding gurus, getting himself around the gyms in order to get the best advice to re-establish himself within the sport. He thanked me for my help, and even sent me a thank-you card on the day of his first come-back show, offering his help, and new found knowledge, for when it came time for me to compete in the later season.

Mark's summer season come-back was a great success, he won the regional qualifier as well as taking a good couple of second/third spots at the Mr England and various UK titles. We were all happy for him as he had seemed a bit down and negative when first returning to the gym. Now he was more confident, more determined than ever. He was pleased with his open season but was a little put out that he hadn't been able to bag a national title, thinking he had deserved at least one. This should have been the end of his season, but now qualified he had decided to take on the British Championships in October, which was also the show I was hoping to qualify for and at the same weight; me and Mark had just become rivals.

At first there wasn't much of a problem. I trained with Z, with Mark joining in with us a couple of times a week. It wouldn't be until after my first qualifier that the rivalry would truly start. I don't think Mark thought I was going to qualify, he spoke to me as if he was the elite and I was still the novice, when that wasn't the case. Even when I was giving advice to people in the gym he would smugly laugh, as if to say what I was saying was nonsense. He seemed to have a problem understanding why I was still more respected than he was throughout the gym. I understood his attitude a bit, as he had just had a great season, and was more educated than I ever would be, well on paper anyway. But this would be the least of my worries, it wouldn't be until I had qualified first time round for the British that the rivalry would seemingly become malicious.

it was dangerous as well as embarrassing when people were looking on, some laughing.

Mark had started working his way into our workouts, which wasn't a problem, but how he took over the spotting would be. Myself and Z had known how to spot each other, with Mark being happy just getting involved, but now he seemed hell-bent on being there for my big sets and soon I would know why. I was throwing some big weights about, edging Mark out on a lot of exercises. This wouldn't be good for him, as he had always been the strong one. By now he could see there wasn't much difference in the size and quality of our physiques, if anything I was a little tighter, but trying to beat me on merit wasn't part of his plan.

Mark initially helped me on dumbbell chest press, which were 70kg in weight. I did my set with him spotting me, but by the end of the set he took one of the weights before I had the chance to balance them, leaving me to fall off the bench, throwing the dumbbell to one side – it was dangerous as well as embarrassing when people were looking on, some laughing. I let it go the first time, but when it happened again, with me thrown from the bench, I started to worry whether there was more to this behaviour than just bad spotting.

The next week or so went by and this time I found myself pinned at the bottom of the squat rack with a 200kg bar bending my spine, again at the hands of Mark. This happened once more under the bench press. Mark knew, I had even said for him to assist me on my first full rep, so when the 150kg bar came off the rack he seemed to have a grip, but then he just let it drop with the bar bouncing off my chest. I was fuming, but in a rage managed to bench around eight reps before flinging the bar down and heading straight out of the gym. I managed to calm down before going back in, then just said to Mark that in future Z would spot me as there were too many mishaps happening. Mark just answered "Yeah, no problem." I thought this would be the end of it, with the problem solved and no need for any argument or fall out. Bear in mind this is only my view of events, there was very little evident at this time.

> "Anyone trying to get the better of me, I will bring them down, no matter what I have to do."

The next week during training Mark said something that came across to me as strange; I wasn't sure whether it was an insight to someone else, or a warning aimed at me. He was staring into the mirror after his set, then out of the blue just said, "Anyone trying to get the better of me, I will bring them down, no matter what I have to do." I didn't know what to make of it at the time, but with everything that had been going on I had become more dubious, if not a little worried.

A week or so went by, and I was ready to progress to the 60kg dumbbell shoulder press. I had Z watching me most weeks up until this point, so when Mark jumped up to spot me, telling Z he'd got it, it was a worry. Being positive I just presumed that he now wanted to redeem himself by giving me a decent spot. As I lifted the dumbbells, his hands were under my triceps where they should be, but he looked preoccupied, and instead of being focused on me he was looking into the other room. Right away I could see this as a mind game set to break my confidence, in the hope that I wouldn't be able to lift the weight, but I carried on regardless. I was now fully ready for a face off if he was about to pull his usual stunt.

As I lifted the weight he lowered his hands with the weight instantly thundering onto my shoulders. Although this was very uncomfortable I managed to lift it back up, if only to prove a point. I managed one more rep, still with no help. Finally, on near completion of the third rep, my arm came down followed by both weights banging down, one of them smashing into the rack as it went. Mark, already realising the outcome, had started walking into the other room. I jumped up and followed him, shouting "What the fuck are you up to?" Mark, quick to think, turned around and said that he couldn't believe I had managed to lift the weight on my own. Now it looked as though he was giving me a compliment. Really he was trying to talk himself out of a heated embarrassing argument, and to a point it had worked, as I had managed to calm down a touch, but I wasn't leaving until I'd had the final word. I quickly thought of a comeback, something to get under his skin. I asked him if I had lifted the weight on my own, which he said I had, still thinking he had cleverly calmed the situation, but then when I calmly said "So that's my personal best then?" I got the reaction I wanted. His eyes rolled over like a shark's. Mark was quite a tough lad, I thought he might go for me as the thought of me beating another of his personal bests would have been eating at him, but he managed to restrain himself on this occasion. This was now a battle of wits, as well as weights, and one I had just won, claiming a new personal best while doing it.

Me and Mark would soon be talking again, it now seemed like he wanted to help me, sharing some of the knowledge that his guru (the guy getting him ready for the show) had passed on to him, as well as stuff he had researched himself. He was, however, trying to talk me more into concentrating on the England show, telling me that the British might not be for me, and that I might be too tall to be competitive as a middleweight. I told him I wasn't bothered, as it was my first time in the Mr's, so as long as I was at my best I would be happy. I knew he didn't really want me there, because he knew it was possible that I could beat him, but hadn't wanted to accept it. I figured that now he wasn't throwing my weights up he couldn't do anything to keep me from the British stage. I could never work out why he was so competitive towards me. If I had been out of things for that long I would have been happy pulling back to the level he was now at, and in such little time.

The Mr England had come, with me unfortunately coming up against the great Harold Pennie, who I thought was going to be the guest poser until seeing him behind me as we walked onto the stage. I was looking my most ripped, and was also at my heaviest. Even though I was outsized by the final two, everyone said I'd looked the most pleasing on stage, they thought my chances at the British were looking good. Mark said the same, but said I could do with being a little more cut, and said I would need to be if I wanted to do well. He mentioned a fat burner called T3, he said if I took ten a day it would get me shredded. He named people, including Matt and other top bodybuilders, saying they all used it, and had used that amount. It seemed a lot, but when he mentioned Matt, I thought it must be OK. I rang Matt just to check, but he was away that week and wouldn't be back until the weekend. I didn't want to limit my chances of success and I only had limited time, so even though I was slightly dubious, I thought it would be OK, I could speak to Matt when he got back, just in case.

After ten days on the T3 I was feeling nauseous, my body was holding water, with my muscles looking like they had shrunk, and even when training I was struggling to get a pump. As soon as I knew Matt was back I was straight on the telephone, telling him about the fat burners, as well as telling him about the amount I had taken. Matt sounded angry, asking me why I hadn't phoned him earlier. When I replied that I had, and that he had been away, he became slightly calmer, then said, "You should have only took half". When I replied, "What, five?", thinking he meant half the amount, Matt, now angry again, said "No, half a tablet!"

He then went on to tell me about the side effects. T3 was a thyroid drug, and with the amount Mark had told me to take not only would it tear down muscle size but, if I had carried on using them right up to the show, when I finally stopped taking them my own thyroid might shut down completely, leaving me prone to putting on a massive amount of weight, never being able to get it off again. My career would have been over, not to mention the fact that I would have been very ill. I realised Matt had got mad because of what might have happened, but he was now calmer, reassuring me that what I had taken wouldn't cause me any damage as long as I came off properly, which I did.

> *He mentioned a fat burner called T3, he said if I took ten a day it would get me shredded.*

I realised Mark had either been given a lot of bad advice or had yet again tried his best to stitch me up. I knew he would have known about the side effects, so even if he was taking this amount, he should still have made me aware of them. This was a lesson learned, so from this year on I wouldn't only research everything I was taking, but would also make sure other less knowing people were also aware, so at least they had the option.

With just a couple of weeks to go, I was fighting to keep hold of the muscle. I looked OK but I knew I wouldn't be at my heaviest, as the T3 effects were still bringing down the weight. I saw Mark in the gym, we hadn't spoken much over the last couple of weeks and now with the show being close, had spoken even less. He was training on his own, looking at himself in the mirror when I first caught a glimpse of his legs. He looked to have cracked it – they looked full and in great condition. But when taking his shirt off I had to question whether he had actually been battering the T3 like he said he had, as his upper body had diminished. His arms and shoulders looked OK, but his back, chest and abs looked like they had virtually vanished, and with little condition to boot. If anyone didn't look ready, it was him.

The night before the contest I was going through my usual preparation. I was shredded, smaller than I wanted to be, but regardless of that was ready to do my best as usual. I was supping a glass of white wine when I heard the phone go, it was Mark telling me he wouldn't be competing, also saying that he wouldn't be there to support me either. It seemed odd, us talking like friends after all the rivalry and fall outs the year had brought; I said I'd ring him to let him know how I got on, and would see him soon. After I came off the phone I felt a bit let down, mainly with myself, as the competition had become more about me and him rather than the competition itself. I had wanted my victory over him, but now, beaten down in both body and mind, I would have to face the Mr Britain, knowing my chances of victory would be slim.

The day arrived and I was once again on stage, back in the thick of it all. I had pumped up better than I expected, but still I was four pounds down on my Mr England best. The top four already seemed in place, I was in the fight between fifth and eighth. I was a little gutted as I knew that without outside influence the story would have been a little different. Matt had shown up to see me compete at the night show, he said I did well to finish where I did; it was good to see him. It had been a success in all, and even though I knew things could have been better, without Matt they could have been a lot worse. It had been a long year, but after the contests everything soon went back to normal. My plans for the next year would be to compete a weight class heavier; I had felt restricted in this class, and for me bodybuilding was about adding muscle in order to sculpt the perfect physique, which I wouldn't be able to do if I was to stick with the middle weight class. Another plus side was that Mark and I would be in separate weight classes, so would have no reason for any further rivalry.

I felt the need to get away this year, so one rainy night in early November I phoned Simon, telling him I had a week off coming up, could I visit him? Si had moved to the US and I couldn't think of a better place to get re-motivated for the oncoming season.

It was just after the September 11th incident and no one wanted to fly to the USA so I could get flight tickets for £100 return. I rang Simon on the Thursday, and by Saturday we were on our way. The trip turned out to be just what we needed. After winning $250 at Atlantic City we could buy all our Christmas presents in New York. We visited the city of Philadelphia where I got to live out one of my childhood dreams of running up the Rocky steps, as well as walking round the streets where the film was made, it was all surreal. We had a good Christmas that year. After a couple of months of filling out and having a clear mind I was now optimistic about the year ahead.

The year started with a boom, me, Z and Mark back training together, hitting it harder than ever, with last year's events now behind us. There was an Ironman event coming up at the start of June, it was a stamina strength contest covering the North West area that had built up a good reputation over the past couple of years. I had always done bodybuilding, so the challenge of a weight-lifting contest was something new. As I had trained using some good weight over the past couple of years, it would be interesting to see how I fared with it when in competition. All of us were training for the event with Mark, Z and Barny going for the 80kg classes, and me aiming for the over 90s.

> *We visited the city of Philadelphia where I got to live out one of my childhood dreams of running up the Rocky steps*

The gym atmosphere had slipped a little over the past year. The place had become a little more gangster, with a lot of name dropping and odd characters appearing. Me and Z weren't arsed about all this, and would always have a scream, taking the piss out of the more serious members, keeping the banter at a high. But when we trained we trained, and myself, Mark, Barny and Z were all renowned for our strength, intense workouts and dedication, with it being balls to the walls now training up to the Ironman contest.

The Ironman came around, we were all in it to win it, and win it we did. Mark and Z placed first and second in their class, I won the heavier weight class, and Barny won the under 80s, making it a clear sweep for Silver's. I also got a personal best on hack squat, managing 250kg, which I had barely been able to do even in practice. Z was slightly put out that Barny had beaten him, in fairness they were a league apart, but we had to say it was close just to keep the peace.

Things were going really well, with the Ironman victory in the bag and my birthday just round the corner. It was my 28th, and with 28 being my favourite number I was hoping it would be a good omen for things to come. We all went out for a meal and it turned out to be a great night, just like I had hoped. Christina brought her friend along to the meal but the friend's husband hadn't been able to come, luckily she ended up hitting it off with Z, enjoying the laughs. Mark, Barny and their girlfriends came as well. It had been my best birthday in a long time and a good final outing before it was time to knuckle down for yet another tough season ahead.

> *The Ironman came around, we were all in it to win it, and win it we did.*

No sooner had my birthday come and gone, with things just starting to look good, when they seemed to be slipping back into last year mode. On the Tuesday, me and Z were pumping up in the gym when the photographer from the local newspaper came down to take our picture with regard to the Ironman contest from the week earlier. Mark had turned up late and was now trying to get a bit of blood into his arms before the shoot. When the photographer was looking for photo ideas Mark was the first to start making suggestions, such as me standing in the middle holding the bar, with him, Z and Barny flexing but looking like they were spotting me. The only problem with this was that holding the bar in this way would make me look narrow, and the fact that Mark had only suggested putting a few plates on the bar wouldn't even suggest that I was particularly strong. At this point I quickly thought back to a year or so earlier when Mark had been kind enough to show me his photo albums. One of the shots showed him and Cyril in jeans doing a double bicep. Mark had said, "Guess whose idea it was to keep the pants on" – knowing Cyril had massive legs and his would have looked small in comparison. With this in mind I now said it how it was, how I hadn't wasted half an hour pumping up to look skinny in the photo and that Mark could do the dead lift in the shot if he wanted to. When he wouldn't, I knew he was just trying it on. He eventually walked off. This incident was something or nothing, but Mark's persistence in always trying to make me look bad in order to make himself look better was never ending.

The next week we were both set to do a photo shoot for a British bodybuilding magazine on the Wednesday. On the Tuesday Mark didn't show up for training. I don't know how, but right away I knew what was going to happen. Wednesday came, and by the night when I had gone in for training I was told that Mark had been in during the afternoon and had done the photo shoot on his own. I had been left out completely, with Mark again giving himself the spotlight.

It wasn't only Mark who had double-crossed me though, Z too had been out to get me but in a more sneaky fashion. Z had been talking to Christina's friend at the birthday meal, he had been telling her about mine and Christina's relationship, saying I was self-righteous, that I thought the world revolved around me. He had also told her about little tricks he would pull in order to get my back up, but most disturbing of all, he had spoken about arguments between Christina and myself, things I had told him in confidence. He then went one step further by saying I had mistreated her, which I never did. I knew I had to address this: if he was telling complete strangers my business who else had he been talking to, and why?

By the weekend I had asked for Z's explanation, he didn't deny anything and when I asked him what had I actually done to make him feel this way, he just looked down at his feet, and said,

"Nothing, you've both been great with me." I felt a little upset for him as I realised he had a bee in his bonnet about both my bodybuilding as well as my relationship, but still I had done everything I could to help him in his training. I had included him in virtually everything good I had ever done so I hadn't deserved this jealous back-stabbing behaviour. I told Z to go away and have a think, then when he was ready to apologise, and meant it, to come round and see me. This never happened, and even though I'd spot him near the house sometimes, he would never knock on the door to apologise like I hoped he would.

Back down the gym I saw Mark and I told him about Z, he said he knew as Z had already told him, then in a blatant manner he said, "I told my Mrs that you and Christina had been falling out, and that you weren't such a perfect couple after all!" – which left me a touch stunned but mainly offended. He proceeded to tell me about all the gyms he had been to, and about how he had been pinned as the number one seed to win both the middleweight and the 85kg British Championships. He started naming names and going on about sponsorship deals; the fact that he hadn't even set foot on a British bodybuilding stage for over 10 years hadn't even crossed his mind. I heard him out before wandering into the now empty-looking gym, and for the first time I saw it for what it was.

To me the gym now looked like an old mill, with a couple of weight machines scattered about... without the atmosphere it once possessed, that's all it was. Mark would have the last laugh on this day. As he entered the gym I had just failed my squat, now climbing out from under the squat rack, I wouldn't even go on to finish my workout. I left the gym on that day with the intention of not going back; this would be hard for me as I had spent 10 years there and had been a big part of the place when at its full glory. Mark, for now, had won, becoming the main man as he obviously wanted.

Mark had told me that he had only helped me out when I was young because he had never seen someone try so hard and gain so little, he never once thought I would get to be as good as I now was. I could see from when he first came back how aware of my reputation he had become, I could see he wanted the same. The only thing I didn't see was that he wanted to be the only one with that reputation, so despite all the help and support I had given him he would show me no remorse nor decency, even after he knew I had left the gym. That night at home I contemplated carrying on, seeing things through at Silver's, but the better part of me knew that the right thing to do was to go, start again elsewhere. Even though I wasn't happy with letting Mark think he had got the better of me, initially wanting a bit of payback, I knew going back wasn't the right thing, being bitter at anyone wasn't going to solve anything. So finally I decided to leave him to it.

the gym now looked like an old mill, with a couple of weight machines scattered about... without the atmosphere it once possessed, that's all it was

Soon I had put these events to the back of my mind, with my heart and mind now focused on getting back into the game, getting into that top five British Final that I so craved. I only had to concentrate on my progress, rather than worry about negative noise affecting the way I thought; Mark and Z had proved themselves to be no more than that, negative noise!

The next day I was off to neighbouring gym Derby's. I didn't know how people would react when I got there, because of the past gym rivalry that had gone on, but to my surprise I was instantly welcomed by no other than Mr Derby himself. Mick was an ex-bodybuilder, strongman and model, but had built his name and wealth mainly through the gym. Derby's was the longest-established gym in town, it was in the basement of a large business building. Mick Derby, Derby's gym, Derby street, mint. The gym was old-school but clean and well-maintained, with plenty of weights within. It was where everyone had started out, and in the old pictures on the wall you could spot a young Sarge, Rob, Ste Harrison and Phil Barber, to mention but a few. Over the weeks Mick told me stories of times gone by, and names now forgotten. Within weeks of being there I had fitted in and felt much happier and able to knuckle down, getting on with my training without any kind of negative input.

My preparation for the 90kg class was going well, but unfortunately I tore the muscle in my left bicep three weeks out. I was able to train around the injury but the muscle was dull in colour, smaller and misshapen so it wouldn't be right for the contest. I knew I had to turn my attention to the 85kg class, British championships, but it turned out that this wasn't happening until the back end of the year. It seemed a long way off. I was just treading water, looking to at least get on stage and compete, but there was more bad news to come. I had been in touch with Matt and heard that while trying to train through his pec tear injury he had used a pain killer which had been addictive, which had led him to a further addiction using stronger drugs. Both Matt and his mum phoned me in the hope that I could help, but I didn't even have a car. Listening to them, and feeling powerless, I knew I would start having driving lessons, as the thought of not being able to help was really getting the best of me. But for now, even though I kept in touch, there wasn't much I could do because of the distances involved with Matt living way out in the valley.

In the void period of time between leaving Silver's and now, my mind-set had changed, I now felt spiritually different. I had always prayed since I was very young, but I was always asking for things, wanting to know why things weren't going right. Although I was still asking God to help Matt, when it came to me I was now thanking God for what I had been able to get through, for seeing the light, avoiding the conflicts and the surrounding hate that seemed to have emerged of late. I felt God had seen me, and he wanted to help, and although I didn't hear voices or have any strange visions, I did feel God was there giving me the answers I had needed, getting me to where I needed to go, giving me some kind of structure once more.

It wouldn't be long before I had selected a show, just to give myself something to work towards. It was a regional show, and I'm not sure why I chose it, but it was in range and at the very least would get me on stage. The training was going well even though I wasn't quite my old self, just taking things one step at a time. My bicep had healed, it was lacking a little definition on the inside where it had torn, but was looking much better. I met some good characters who would show their support, with the most noted being a guy named Amos.

Amos was the main guy at the gym, he was renowned for his amazing condition, but it was his amazing dieting stories I would best remember him for. He would tell of getting some guy to drive him up to the moors then how he would have to walk back without any food or money. In another story he locked himself

I was now thanking God for what I had been able to get through, for seeing the light

in a room for three days so he couldn't eat anything. He was like a nutty professor with crazy theories which fortunately for him, would work. His stories were great, and always made me laugh as he told them with such enthusiasm. The other guy was Jim Moore, who would tell me of his past bodybuilding career, he told me how he had been involved in a bad car accident that had put his career on hold for the past five years. Jim was the first person from Derby's I would motivate back into competition, he said that after seeing me he had wanted to return to the stage, and a year later, he did. His wife didn't like me for a while.

The day of the show came round with me eager to get on stage. Christina and I got to the venue and were greeted by Amos and a lad named Adie Pierce who had come to watch. I was happy because I hadn't been at Derby's long and I hadn't expected anyone to come. But the next face I saw didn't quite have the same impact. Mark was there and madly enough came over and sat near us as if nothing had ever gone on. He made it known he knew a few people, and had even told his main competition on the day how he was Number One. I knew I was already a better person, so wasn't bothered; his words meant nothing now, I had no hate towards him like I thought I might. We were in separate classes, with Mark being the upper weight in his class, and me in the lower weight of the heavier weight class. With him up first, it was time to see what all the fuss was about.

> Roger's pictures, as well as his complimentary ways, had got my head right

As he came on stage, I saw that although he was bigger, he didn't look as good as I had expected him to, but I wondered whether he would still get the title through the people he knew. I kind of smiled but felt a bit sad at the same time, mainly due to our past friendship. It was now time to see whether the judges thought the same or whether I had missed something in the way that I'd judged him.

The top three names came in, but Mark wasn't there, only placing fourth. His face told you everything you needed to know. In fairness, he should have made the top three. I didn't see him after this. When my class came on, despite being surrounded by heavyweights, I still managed to hit the top three, getting to take home a trophy. That night I wondered why I had chosen that show. I thought that perhaps God had wanted me to see the demise of my former rival, and in some way wanted to do to him as he had done to me, God showing me he was on my side.

Two weeks on, I went on to win a regional qualifier. It was good to have one new victory under my belt. Back in the gym, training was now picking up, even more so with the focus on my next venture. I thought that if I could hold out for another three weeks then organise a photo shoot, I would at least have been on stage as well as have some photos, making it a worthwhile year, but I was still really hoping to be able to get to the British final as originally planned. Taking one step at a time, whilst training up to smaller events, would keep me more focussed. I trained right up to the photo shoot, seeing it as if it was a show.

I had overcome the spell that had put a negative void in my life

At the photo shoot I was greeted by Roger Shelley, a photographer with a worldwide reputation, he had photographed Dorian Yates and Berry de Mey to mention but a few. Roger had always done my photos but he seemed more impressed with me this year, comparing me to some of my all-time idols, the likes of Bob Paris and the legendary Frank Zane. After the shoot he showed me some of the shots on his PC and I was more than happy with what I saw. I think my self-confidence had been affected with the past goings-on, but now Roger's pictures, as well as his complimentary ways, had got my head right. Once again I felt confident in how I looked, now ready to take on the trek of training that would lead me to the British final.

As soon as Monday hit the decision was in, I was heading for the Britain. I was getting stronger, training faster, and had overcome the spell that had put a negative void in my life. The last five weeks are normally the worst, but this time it felt like easy street. When I was out on my post round everyone was seeing me in shape, some asking about the show. My pal Earthy from the shop where I had my bags dropped was also helping out, plying me with black coffee, bottles of water and chewing gum, he said that he and his brothers wanted to contribute so that when I won they could say they had helped. All the young girls were smiling, being giddy when passing me on the street, with the likes of Jim, Amos, Mick and the two Aidys always being positive yet honest when viewing me at the gym. I had managed to bring back the year.

For the couple of days before the show I could put my feet up. I was now able to carb up properly, whilst watching my favourite motivational movies, drinking water or black coffee. I felt pretty content up to the final night, but the night before the contest, I started to feel nervous. Was I good enough to make the top five? What if I didn't get placed?

I went into a panic, the pressure had got to me, I started ranting, "I can't do it, I can't do it!" I had become frantic. Christina was trying to calm me down, and although shocked by the outburst, she managed to get me sat down, reassuring me that I was going to do well. But when she said she had a feeling I was going to win, I cracked up even more, ranting about her jinxing me just by saying it. It was all a bit mad but it had got me really upset.

WHEN SHE SAID SHE HAD A FEELING I WAS GOING TO WIN, I CRACKED UP EVEN MORE, RANTING ABOUT HER JINXING ME JUST BY SAYING IT

Where the Hell did he come from?

CHAPTER 14

The Mr Britain

The morning of the show came, and it was almost like the night before hadn't happened; I was feeling ready to take on the day, feeling good about what I was about to present. The day seemed to move pretty fast, before I knew it I was backstage with the rest of my class, all ready to pump up. There were a lot of big names, just as you would expect from a British final. I knew most of the names in the line-up, and was well aware that a lot of them had won big contests. There were a lot of big gestures, with everyone trying to frighten each other in the way they spoke and sold themselves; it was all pretty mad.

When I took my shirt off, I could see I was already looking full, even before pumping up. My legs were more cut, notably bigger than ever before, so just with this I was happy, I knew I was going to be looking my best as well as being competitive. I was barely noticed when I started to pump up, but within ten minutes I looked nearly twice the size, with masses of vascularity bounding all over my chest, arms and shoulders, with all of the competitors now looking at me as if to say, where the Hell did he come from? The carbing up had more than worked, and by the time I got out onstage it looked as if I had been blown up with a bicycle pump, with the transformation nothing short of freaky.

Onstage I was instantly in the firing line with my name being called out for comparisons. As time went on I was taking centre stage more and more, being called out with a lot of the bigger names, it was a blast. There weren't many people there to support me, but my little sister Debra and Christina were making that much noise you would have thought that I had brought an army with me. When I left the stage I felt happy with the callouts as well as the day so far. As I got off stage the official said I was back for the night show, this could only mean one thing, I had made the final five. I was over the moon as that was my initial goal at the start of the year, but I was now wondering if I had done enough to challenge for the final three.

There was more room backstage at the night show so had a bit of breathing space, and everyone was a little more relaxed knowing that the judging had been done. I was getting tanned up by both Christina and Debra when one of the guys said, "It's worth turning up just for that!" with everyone laughing and making light, but soon it would be time to get serious as it was now nearly time to step back out on stage that one last time. We were all in line, I knew I was the least known on this day, with the crowd yelling out the names of who they thought should win. Different names shouted by different crowds, but then I would hear Christina and Debra shouting "Go on John! John McLough number one!", in their crowd of two, which I found really funny as they were both around seven stone, pissed through.

The crowd was asked for quiet as the final scores came in. The fifth place was announced, and wasn't me. Already I was thinking I had placed higher here than in any other British championship to date. Then fourth, then third – my name still not said. Now I was nervous. There were only two of us left, and one of us was about to be crowned British Champion. After getting that far, I really wanted the title.

The second place was in – and it wasn't me. I hit the roof, total disbelief; I had come in the underdog and had taken the title! My fist clenched, I shouted "Fucking yes! Number one!" What a moment it was, and what a journey it had been, there were cheers, boos and all sorts of comments being thrown (the southerners weren't the best losers!), but still you couldn't get me off that stage, I posed on like a mad man, I had waited too long to now leave quietly, it was a triumphant moment, one of my most cherished memories.

I went on to do my first overall, this is where all the weight class winners come together to decide who's 'best of the best' on the evening, with the final three able to compete in the Mr Universe. A guy named Paul George took the title on this evening, and rightly so, his shape was immense with his condition freaky, he actually looked to have been slashed with a knife, his midsection was that cut. Kevin Alder and Bryan Connolly were also part of the overall, both looking immense. As I got in that night I couldn't stop laughing, even when I went to bed I still I couldn't stop. I ended up going downstairs and sitting up all night giggling like a child, it was fierce.

I ended up going downstairs and sitting up all night giggling like a child, it was fierce.

This had been the greatest moment of my bodybuilding career, but what it had taken to get there made the victory feel even more spectacular. That night as I sat awake I felt totally happy; a rare moment for anyone. I thanked God for his blessing, also thankful he had watched over me. I realised at this point that every step of my early life had been based around the church, from when I first learned to ride a two-wheeled bike, having to climb on the church steps just to get on. The church was also where I first danced in front of a large crowd, after I had practiced all summer, right through to where I would build structure and responsibility, setting up and running the youth clubs in my mid-teens. God had always known and watched out for me, but it had taken until now for me to get to know him in the same way.

With the show over, the world felt like a better place. I was greeted with handshakes, hugs and kind words from the lads at the gym, as well as friends at work. I got my picture and story in the paper, which was the first time I had been in the paper with me as the only focus. Earthy had stuck my picture up in the front of his shop, so now everyone in the area knew who I was, and what I had won. Trucks and cars would beep when I was out on my round, shouts of "Champion!" and other pleasantries to do with what I had just won, I soon realised that all the guys I used to help out still remembered me. The young girls on my round would all give me smiles. It wasn't until the last girl passing said, "He's white this week" that I realised they hadn't fancied me or thought me cool at all, they had just noticed me doused in different shades of tan most weeks and probably just thought I was some weird fucker who liked putting fake tan on at weekends. Even though embarrassed, I still found this funny.

For the next four or five months I felt like the king of the world. I was British champion, no one could ever take that away from me.

For the next four or five months I felt like the king of the world.

I never allowed myself much let up after the show and even less when the New Year came in. Early into the year 2003 I had wanted to use my titles to build a career, so was already studying to be a fitness trainer as well as taking sports nutrition at diploma level. I wasn't going to compete in bodybuilding this year because I wanted to work more on power, then later on stamina strength, working up to do some Ironman shows, as this would give me a focus point. I also knew that if I was concentrating on doing bodybuilding contests I wouldn't get through my exams. I still needed to improve with my bodybuilding because even though I had won the Britain, when it came to the overall placings I hadn't finished in the final three, which I needed to do in order to compete internationally with this Federation.

I applied for a string of jobs in the fitness industry, thinking that with my experience and titles, I would be snapped up, and able to work on building a career doing what I did best. I had three Ironman contests lined up for the early summer, the second Ironman was taking place at my former hang-out, Silver's gym. But first I was out to pound out some weight whilst hitting a few personal bests as I went.

My first training partner bailed on me as he thought that competing at Silver's in the Ironman would be a death trap. Since my show, there were lots of rumours flying about that Mark was upset about my title, ranting about giving me a crack next time he saw me. Another rumour was that he and his posse were coming round to smash my house up as well as break my knees. I wasn't sure what was true or hearsay, but it made me want to go and do the show even more. My training partner, thinking I was nuts, went his own way, leaving my mate from Silver's, Andy Whittle, to take his place.

After both back and leg workouts we always ended up sitting down, pale-faced, unable to speak

Andy was a big strong lad. I had always thought when at Silver's that he was an off-season bodybuilder, but as it turned out he was a former powerhouse martial artist. He had come across from Silver's when I left in order to help me out up to my show, but unfortunately I had been too snappy when he was spotting me, so we decided I had best train alone up to the show in order to keep our friendship. But now there were no shows so we could get together, hitting it hard. I hit a lot of my all-time personal bests that year, including a 200kg bench, 200kg bent over row and a dead lift of 280kg, with Andy hitting a lot of PBs too whilst coming into good shape. After both back and leg workouts we always ended up sitting down, pale-faced, unable to speak to each other as the workouts were so heavy and intense. Sometimes we just ended up sprawling across the floor semi-passed out and semi-unable to breathe properly, it was all pretty mad.

Unfortunately my search for jobs in the fitness trade wasn't going so well. After several interviews there were still no openings. The gyms seemed to want novices, with the more honest interviewers telling me that the interview had been great but, with what I had done and knew, it wouldn't feel right them telling me to wipe down machines, or clean the mirrors, out of respect for me.

The other, more typical excuse was that management feared for their own jobs, not wanting me there regardless of what I could do for their business. On the training front, I had just won my first of the season Ironman contests, and it was now time for me to compete at the Ironman in my home town.

The Bury Ironman competition had come, and despite people telling me it was a bad idea I had decided to do it. I had also decided that when I entered Silver's I would go in on my own. As I entered, the gym was packed full of energy. I was instantly greeted with friendly faces, faces I had known from when I last trained there. I stood and exchanged pleasantries for a while, then was asked by the new owner Joe if I would sign in at the back. As I went in the back room it was Barny who was signing everyone in, but Mark was there also. There was no kind greeting or smile, but neither would there be any kind of attack from him or anyone else. I knew then that by just turning up, there would be no more said, as whoever had been spreading the rumours would have had ample opportunity to get me if they had wanted to. I walked back out unscathed for all to see.

The show commenced with me competing in the super heavyweight division, trying to take on the big boys. I didn't get off to the greatest start as I nearly tripped whilst walking to the squat rack with 200kg on my back, but luckily this didn't affect my performance as I managed around 12 reps which was pretty good by my standards. Again, on the dead lift, I had suffered a minor tear a few weeks earlier so I was supposed to be cautious, but come the day I just went for it and although I did OK I had to drop the bar early, as I felt a massive spasm between my triceps and deltoids where I'd had the initial tear. After this event I threw my guts up outside, yet when I returned for the next event I put in a stellar performance on the bench press, as well as taking the next two events, which brought me back into the contest. I was now happy with my overall performance.

There was only one winner on the day, a guy named Alvin Isherwood, he was doing 35 reps on virtually everything, making this contest look more like his everyday workout. Alvin was a good guy, he was the best stamina strength athlete I ever saw. I managed joint third but wouldn't be awarded the trophy, or even mentioned, and couldn't be bothered finding out whether I had counted up right or whether it had just been overlooked when it had come to the scoring. I had done what I had come to do, so was just happy catching up with all the guys who had come to support me. My old pal Barny took the under 80kg title on this day and I think Mark finished second in the class above.

> *The left side of my back and arm was completely black.*

This would be the last time Mark would compete, with his last bodybuilding show being the one I had seen him in earlier in the year. It was a shame, as we had been such good friends, he had given me a lot of inspiration and we shared a lot of laughs. It was Mark who had helped to build me, both mentally and physically, early doors, he had helped build my world, but in the end he wouldn't want me on the same planet, he seemed like a completely different person to the good natured lad I was once close with. The guy had been a hero to me when first starting out.

A week went by, with me having to keep an eye on the left side of my chest as it had become massively bruised due to the contest – I was a little worried. I asked Christina to come into the bathroom to see what she thought. As soon as she came in her face dropped, and that was followed by a loud scream. I quickly took a look then said it wasn't that bad, but she was just pointing to my back, now virtually in tears. The left side of my back and arm was completely black. Instantly I knew it was a bad tear, but I wasn't sure exactly where the muscle had torn as the full half of my back was totally black in colour. I'd seen this kind of bruising one too many times on friends in the past, so was now thinking the worst.

LIVING THE NIGHTMARE **BECOMING THE DREAM**

Within the week I was taken into hospital. It turned out that the back of my shoulders had pulled away from the tricep, distorting the shape as well as tearing a massive amount of fibre from both my shoulder and arm, it was lucky I hadn't torn the muscle completely off. The doctor worked on it by shooting biodegradable pins into my armpit, which would hold the triceps and shoulder muscle together to let it reform as I recovered. Recovery time would be four to eight weeks.

It didn't take long until I started to feel a bit down on my luck, with the whole of the past couple of years now coming back to haunt me. I felt I needed to let loose, have a couple of drinks, a few good times perhaps, to see how the other half lived whilst I was unable to do anything else. Unfortunately, me and drink didn't mix so this would only end up making matters worse.

I went out three out of the four weeks in the first month following my injury and ended up getting involved in lots of bother, may have even taken drugs, I'm not sure, I don't remember much being honest, I was fucked, I know that much. I was getting into fights even though I could only use one arm! Don't think I won any. People were seeing me in a different light, telling me bits and bobs of what they had seen and heard, but it was my little sister Debra and cousin Phil seeing me off my face that would upset me the most. Neither of them had seen this side to me in a long time, they were worried, I'd only wanted to have a good time. This was the last time I ever drank, it wasn't a pleasant time but was a good wake up call, it showed me what I was meant to be and what I wasn't meant to be.

Life had also become stressful at home, myself and Christina were arguing a lot more due to my aggressive manner and odd behaviour. Making things worse, we had new neighbours who had started dragging all their mates over from Ireland for barmy weekend parties, so the house was constantly noisy, and from Thursday to Sunday was always full of pissheads. Not only that but through the day some

124

maintenance guy was coming round doing odd jobs, using drills and hammers. Even though I had tried talking to them both nicely, trying to find a compromise, nobody seemed to listen and it all just carried on regardless. Basically I was getting no sleep, I couldn't train, and I was now paranoid about how I had been on my nights out. In the midst of it all, myself and Christina were no longer a tight unit, we were yelling at each other and occasionally smashing the house to bits, my stress levels hitting the roof.

After around five weeks my arm had recovered to a decent level, I was back in the gym but only lifting light. There was still no luck on the trainer job front, so with both of us feeling fed up we started talking about emigration, selling the house and trying to get into the USA. I was still trying my best to reduce my stress levels, but whilst still on one I wanted to deal with these neighbours of mine as well as the maintenance guy.

First I saw to the maintenance man who had become more arrogant than ever, he had stupidly mistaken my kindness for weakness. It wasn't until I was rattling the fucker off his ladder that he finally realised just how pissed at him I was. Same again with the neighbours; come Saturday night when the party was at its loudest, I walked into their house and pushed a guy into the TV stand before kicking fuck out of the wall stereo, bringing an end to their party season. I had only myself left to sort out now, so decided a total detox was in order; I started to eat soft broccoli and egg-white with plenty of warm water and zero caffeine in-between. I was only going to do this for four or five weeks, but because of how well I felt from it I decided to stick with it right up until Christmas.

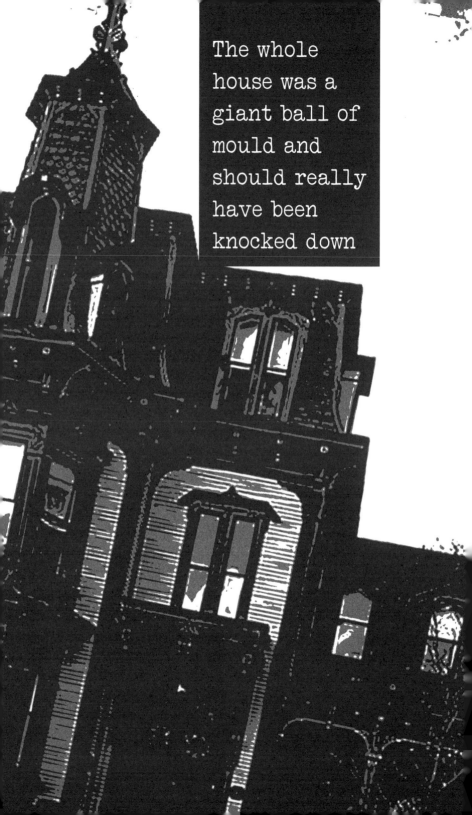

The whole house was a giant ball of mould and should really have been knocked down

CHAPTER 15

The house from hell

By the start of 2004 we had managed to sell the house but unfortunately immigration into the USA would prove more difficult than we had first thought, with even Christina's midwifery qualification not enough to get us in. The US would only recognise paediatric nurses, which was another two-year training course which Christina would have to do. And since 9/11 it was much harder to get in on a permanent visa, regardless. We had decided to move in with my cousin, in order to save on rent, but this wasn't working out too good either and before long my cousin and Christina were having fallouts with me stuck somewhere in the middle.

My stress levels were rising once more as I realised that we weren't getting any further with our plan of getting to the US. I had been studying for the past two years with my exams now in sight but was now playing referee with no compromise on either side. Luckily I would get through my exams, able to pass with flying colours, but I was a little pissed about everything that had gone on.

Somehow my mum and dad got involved, and then I knew it was time to leave, as I didn't want them getting stressed with it all. We quickly viewed a few properties and found one we both liked, it was an old terrace but Christina liked the way it had been decorated with it looking modern and new from the inside. The house also appealed to me because it was only two minutes from work and 10 minutes from the gym, so was a win-win either way. The only problem now was getting our stuff from my cousin's, as she had changed the locks and given us allocated times when to collect our things, which didn't help matters much.

Another problem at this time was the big changes that were going on at work. A new way of working had just come into play, the mail needed to be sorted faster and our deliveries were lengthened, which led to a lot of anger amongst staff. A lot of things were said.

I went into the office to try and put things right. What happened next I won't go into, I will say things got a little out of hand. I was asked to leave the building, and was later told I was suspended without pay due to violent/aggressive behaviour; this in turn meant my job was now on the line. Within the day Christina was on the phone talking to higher management trying to put things right, trying to calm the situation with my interests at heart. I wasn't in the clear, but 'matters would be looked into' as to whether I would keep my job or not, with the outcome at the time looking quite bleak.

I was sent to a neighbouring town whilst things were being sorted, I would have to work in the office as I was being monitored on my behaviour and temperament, although I didn't know this at the time. In the first couple of weeks I had already been involved in a fall-out, which ended up with me chasing some cheeky fucker round the building in a fit of rage. Luckily for me this guy was renowned for his behaviour, so when I was once more in the office explaining my side of the story to the management, I would be given another chance. I felt at ease as the manager there had seemed fair, and fair I could deal with. There were no more problems after this, instead I would keep my head down, be polite and work hard. Even in my break I kept busy, revising my driving theory test so I wouldn't involve myself with any outside conversation, or know of anyone else's business except my own. So my working life was OK, I was left alone.

Life on the home front wasn't so great, as getting into the US now seemed impossible, and the house we had rented was starting to cause Christina some concern. She was constantly complaining to me about a damp smell, which wasn't much of a problem, but it was when she started mentioning tiny ugly insects appearing everywhere that I started to worry. At first I was worried about Christina's mental state, and thought that because of all our past problems she had started to go a bit nuts. She was talking about little insects appearing in her clothes, on the bed, and even in her hair dryer, but when I came to look there was nothing there. Coming home from work I would find her looking up at the walls, noticing the damp spots becoming more apparent, talking about bugs taking over the house, to the point it had become all she would talk about. I didn't really take her on, I was only interested in my next meal and getting to the gym.

> I didn't really take her on, I was only interested in my next meal

Weeks went by with Christina spending a lot more time at her mum's, or out with friends, with me spending more and more time at the gym as I was now starting to prepare for my next competitive season. No bugs, mad women or job loss was going to stand in my way. As it turned out Christina wasn't going mad and managed to bag one of her little friends in a jar, and after I'd seen the first one, the rest started to show their ugly little faces. I was going through my wardrobe one day when I noticed that all the bottoms of all my shirts had holes in them. As I looked more closely, I could see the shirts were riddled with these horrible little creatures. Even worse, while throwing all my clothes into a bin bag I could see that they had eaten through the back of the wardrobe, and behind the wardrobe was a huge damp hole where they were breeding. I felt like I was in some grossed out horror movie. I got onto the landlord, telling him he needed to deal with the problem, he said he would sort it, but even though various people would come around to do bits of jobs, nothing would make any difference. The whole house was a giant ball of mould and should really have been knocked down. While this was all going on Christina seemed on the brink of some kind of breakdown and was spending more time at her mum's, sometimes spending a couple of days at a time stopping over at her house.

It was my 30th birthday, and even though birthdays weren't really my thing I thought with this being a big one that someone would have planned a bit of something for me, especially with the kind of year I'd had, but this wasn't to be. I came home from work expecting some kind of surprise, but Christina had been too caught up with the bug infestation and had forgotten to do anything, neither had anyone else, nor had anyone been in touch to send their regards. I went up to my mum's later that day only to find out that no one was in, my birthday had been totally forgotten. To cheer myself up I thought I would run home to test my fitness, to see if I was still as fit as I had been when I was 20, so I did a five-mile dash back home. I realised I still had good stamina and could run like fuck if I wanted to. This was the only positive I would have on this day.

no one was in, my birthday had been totally forgotten

A few months went by, nothing much changed, other than my relationship decaying at a massive rate and more people from work saying they didn't think I would get my job back because of how long I had been away. Only a handful of people stayed in touch, the main two being my long-term friend Julie and the manager from work, Steve. I heard both were fighting my corner when anything negative was said about me, with Julie picking the best duty for me, making sure I wasn't passed over in the reselection for when I hopefully returned.

The only thing going in the right direction at this time was my training. I had stayed 100% focused, I even thought, if it all goes wrong and I lose my job, my house, my wife, or even my mind, I was going to make sure that before hitting rock bottom I would compete, making what might be my last year, my best. Fortunately for me it wouldn't come to that, but still my attitude whilst training for contests from that year on would be to treat each competitive season as if it was my last. I would always play my best hand, never leaving any cards on the table (not that I ever had).

By September of that year I had persuaded the landlord from Hell to terminate the letting contract. Christina and I could now move on and, with no big move to the USA, we had bought and were settling into a new house, our relationship slowly starting to improve. The news was also in about whether or not I kept my job, and the news was good – although I received a five-year suspended dismissal I was able to go back to work, but had to avoid getting into any type of trouble in the time period set. It was

> *I had clung on to the one thing I could control and make good*

manager Steve Hardman who had convinced the powers that be to give me a second chance, and I'll always be thankful to both him and Julie for sticking by me throughout the whole diabolical affair.

Derby's had closed its doors after 20 long years, so it was now time to return to Silver's. When I returned I was greeted by a guy called Chris who said he had heard of me but had never met me in person. Joe had done a good job of turning the 'fitness centre' back into a gym. I asked about Mark and was told he had been banned only a month earlier, I won't go into it. I thought the story was funny, if not a bit mad, but I was glad of the way it had turned out because now all I would have to worry about was getting it right for my upcoming contest.

My main contest soon came around. This year I was to be competing in the medium height class at the British Final 2004. When the day of the show came, despite the ridiculous year I'd had, I had still managed to prepare for this show better than any other, as while most other aspects of my life had been bad, I had clung on to the one thing I could control and make good.

As I went on stage to compete I was aware that I had lost a little condition in my legs due to the cold floors backstage, and it wasn't until midway through the callouts that the condition returned, but along with everyone else I thought I had the contest in the bag as my overall size, condition and shape was far superior to my nearest rival. I posed with grace and confidence, and was enjoying the crowd's response, and even though I had kept my head down while preparing for the show there was still a great turn out of supporters from the gym, which I was thankful for. I was enjoying being back on stage at both my heaviest and sharpest to date. The judges' scores came in, it was a deadlock, a tie for first place. I wasn't sure how this would work, but then to my great surprise the commentator said that both of the winners would have to fight it out at the Mr Universe! I was over the moon, now I would be going to the Mr Universe, competing for the world title, my first time on the world stage.

I was over the moon, now I would be going to the Mr Universe

During the few weeks between the shows I would have to cancel a few arrangements. I wouldn't be able to go to Simon's wedding and had to cancel our holiday, but Simon and Christina both understood, they knew just how much this meant to me. I couldn't let it go, always keeping in my head Big Lee's words of not just presuming that there was going to be another chance, as well as my own new perception of seeing every competition like it would be my last. Unlike a lot of people I was pretty good at talking myself into things rather than making excuses not to do them, I could have easily used plenty of excuses with everything I had been through that year.

The time had come for us to take a flight overseas to what would be my first international contest. Somehow we got talking to a couple who we instantly got close with. He was a big guy named Nigel who would be competing in the Men's Tall Class, and for the duration we were there we spent most our time together with his wife and mine.

The night before the show I got very nervous due to the incident where my legs had struggled to come through. I ended up sleeping in the bath with my legs elevated, massaging the water out of them. I was constantly posing them, making sure they remained cut, driving myself and Christina mad having to turn the lights on to check the mirror. I remembered seeing Matt do this several years earlier, and thinking he was a bit nuts, now here I was doing exactly the same thing, but in the middle of the night.

As I went out on stage the audience was immense and the atmosphere electric

The big day had arrived, I was raring to go. Myself and Nigel would help each other backstage. I was happy with how I looked, but even more glad that my legs had remained in good condition. The backstage was packed, so initially I didn't expect much, as everyone looked good when lining up to be viewed. As I went out on stage the audience was immense and the atmosphere electric. I didn't get any early call outs but in the latter end of the pre-judging I was called out on three occasions, which I was happy with first time out at such an event, I knew that I had done better than some, as many hadn't been called out at all.

After coming off stage I was told I had got through into the final ten so would be going through to the night show, as well as being in the running for the final six split. I was looking forward to the presentation, already feeling glad to be part of the top 10 as I had thought that only the final six, or final three, would be placed. The night show came around with each country having its national anthem played, I stood on stage hand on heart as ours played out, I then got to wave the British flag before leaving the stage to a roar of applause. I've got to say I felt very proud at this moment, I was glad to be a representative of my country, to be part of something this big. I went on stage for the final placing and was announced for placing ninth. I was happy with the outcome, and realised that I had done a little bit more than just make up the numbers. I thought the result was fair but at the same time I knew I hadn't been outclassed, I had just made my first positive step into the international arena, and I'd enjoyed every minute of it.

> *I had done a little bit more than just make up the numbers*

Back to reality, it was good to get back to Silver's. Joe congratulated me, giving me free membership for doing well for the gym, as I was starting to bring in new members. It wasn't long before me and Joe found ourselves working on the same door together, so ended up becoming quite good friends. I was once again well-received, and respected by the older members of the gym as well as the new more hungry up-comers, it seemed like I'd never been away.

At home things weren't so good. Christina and I weren't seeing eye-to-eye. The stress of the year had come to a head, and arguments over whose fault it all was, and why we hadn't got into America were all being brought up. So over the Christmas period of 2004 we separated, as we seemed to have different ideas about what being in a relationship was about.

Into the new year 2005, and while being separated I upped my nights on the door to three, and took on a rigorous mid-week mixed martial arts class, as I wanted to stay leaner in my off-season as well as be on top of my game as a doorman. Luckily by doing this I left myself very little energy to worry about what was going on in my relationship, even though I still wanted to get things back to the way they were as soon as I could. I needed to clear my mind of the year gone by, as did Christina, so I think the time apart was good, if only for that reason.

By March 2005 we were meeting up trying to resolve our differences. The first two meetings didn't go well, we couldn't reach a compromise or sort anything out, but the third meeting went well and we decided to give it another go. It wouldn't be long before our relationship had picked up, as we were now settling nicely into our new surroundings, enjoying life in suburbia, as well as making friends with our new neighbours, including one of my old best friends Dozer who I had worked the door with in years gone by. It was the fresh start Christina and I had needed, and we were now both able to enjoy being together once more.

I HAD JUST MADE MY FIRST POSITIVE STEP INTO THE INTERNATIONAL ARENA, AND I'D ENJOYED EVERY MINUTE OF IT

Europe beckons for weightli[...]

● MUSCLEMEN LIFT TITLES: Winning bodybuilding duo John McLoughlin (left), and Alex Clark [...]

John McLoughlin

7 SEPTEMBER 2015

MR UNIVERSE
TITLE FOR [...]

"Oh my word, this guy could
be the next big thing."

CHAPTER 16

My new apprentice

Down the gym I was bringing in new members, with quite a few of them being my own clients, as I was now up and running with my own personal training business. My clients were getting in shape fast, achieving good results with how I trained them. This year I was be introduced to a young lad by the name of Alex Clarke. Alex was a young, keen up-comer who wanted to get into bodybuilding, he was looking for advice. One of the lads in the gym sent him my way, so I agreed to help him out, as he was only 15 and I didn't want him getting influenced by the wrong people. First, I had a look at him to see what potential he had, and even at first glance I instantly thought, "Oh my word, this guy could be the next big thing." He was already in good shape with good muscle maturity as well as a decent amount of thickness for such a young lad. As we sat down, I told him to sit closer so he could hear me properly, so he pulled his chair up until he was about an inch away from my face. I had to ask him to move back a little because at that range I was worried that people looking on would think we were about to kiss, which wouldn't be good, and even worse as he was wearing a school uniform at the time. I think Alex thought I was a little too intense on the first chat, but I wanted him to know that if I was going to mentor him there would be no messing about, and that I didn't have the time nor energy to spend on fools or time wasters. This would be the first time I had trained anyone right from scratch, so I wanted to make sure I did a good job, and get the young lad's career off to a good start, with no mess-ups like I had made in my earlier years.

It was good to spend time with Alex, being able to pass on my knowledge. I enjoyed the role of trainer, especially because how he would look on stage would reflect on me and what I knew to be right. Alex did well this first year, he had come in top condition, and with the advice and help I had given him he gained a lot of muscle but also had great balance and shape with it. Only sixteen years old at the time of his first shows, he had to go up against guys up to 21 years of age, but still with the four shows he did he never once placed outside of the top three.

I DIDN'T HAVE THE TIME NOR ENERGY TO SPEND ON FOOLS OR TIME WASTERS.

it was now my turn

CHAPTER 17

Risking life and limb just to get on stage

I had been getting people into good shape throughout the first part of the year, but it was now my turn, with me once more out to prove my worth in the bodybuilding arena. I had spent the earlier part of the year training with Dozer, my old door mentor, but now it was coming closer to contest I would opt to train on my own. For cardio I mainly used the stationary bike, as it had easy-to-work settings and the seat was built with the shorter person in mind. Unfortunately the seat was very uncomfortable so when peddling hard it would take the skin off the tops of my legs which would sometimes crease, leaving me to walk out of the gym bow-legged. Myself and Jim Moore (my old pal from Derby's gym) were in the cardio room most days, which worked out well as both of us being victims of low-carb diets, there was little need for conversation. We would mutter along to each other in the first five minutes, in language only the two of us could understand, before switching off, then carrying on with our cardio session, both usually grunting, pissed through with cold sweat, smelling like old boots by the end of our workouts.

Jim and I had planned to do the same shows, with the first one being the UK Championships 2005, this would be our run-through show. This first show was the one you did when you were low in carbs, it could be used as an opener but one you wouldn't bother peaking for. The second show, the British, was the show you would put everything into in order to win so you could get through to the Universe. I was lucky this year as all the top ten from last year's Mr Universe had already qualified, so even if I didn't qualify at the British this time around I would still have the option to compete at the Mr Universe again. Being honest I would want to compete at both if possible.

The months went by and preparation for this year's shows had gone well so before I knew where I was, it was more or less time to compete. I had recently passed my driving test, so thought I would drive us both down to the show, as Jim didn't have a car and both our wives were working on that day so couldn't make it. I'd driven on the normal roads a couple of times but this was the first time I had driven on the motorway, and because of the low carbs, my mind wasn't on the job. I didn't realise the speed I was going, and I wasn't concentrating too hard on how the lanes were marked out, so kept on driving in-between them. I kept slipping in and out of day-dreams, being inattentive when driving, other drivers pipping me from time to time, bringing me back round, swerving dangerously to get back in the lane I should have been in. I looked at Jim, he looked pretty terrified, so eventually I had to tell him that I was struggling to keep focused and that this was the first time I had driven any kind of distance and on this kind of road.

Jim, being the gent he was, then volunteered to take over the driving, so at first I thought 'problem solved', but when we were back on the road I asked him why he didn't drive, and he came back with an answer I wasn't quite expecting. With the car now at full speed he said he had had his licence taken from him as he had suffered with seizures, so couldn't drive any more. I asked him if he was now all right could he not get his licence back, and he replied that he was not all right, "I still have blackouts, I could pass out at any second." I looked at the road, then at Jim, then blurted out, "What the fuck are you doing driving my car then?" Jim said he hadn't suffered any blackouts for a while, but all through the journey I was watching his hands and the way he was driving, knowing that I might have to grab the wheel at the drop of a hat. To make matters worse, we missed our turning and drove practically all the way to Wales before we turned back, making the journey twice as long with a guy who could pass out at any second still driving the car. I wanted to take over, but I didn't have a clue where we were, and as I was now mega pale-faced with fright I would probably have been just as dangerous as my crazy friend at the side of me.

The trip seem to take a lifetime, I think we drove through the same nearby town around six times before reaching our final destination. We ended up getting to the show just as the doors were opening, and by the time we had parked up the queue had gone so we could get straight in and through to backstage without any messing about. Jim was in the Masters, his class first on stage. I had been too preoccupied trying to get a decent spot to realise that Jim only had five minutes

"I'm knackered and I'm hungry."

with us still having to get his tan on. I quickly tried slapping on as much as I could, but it was too late, he would have to go on stage looking like a half-cooked piece of chicken. I felt really guilty whilst waiting for his class to come off stage, I knew the bad time management had been my fault.

Jim finally came off stage looking totally fed up, but I realised he had been in the trophies so hadn't walked away empty-handed. When I asked him how he had got on, he said he had actually won; but he was still looking totally fed up, then just said, "I'm knackered and I'm hungry." Then we both just laughed, realising how far gone we both were.

Just before my class was called back I was sitting on the floor, calling to Jim, Jim was shouting back asking where I was, but was staring up at the ceiling semi-docile, it was like a bad comedy show, we were both absolutely knackered.

It was my turn next and when pumping up I realised the other lads in my class hadn't turned up in great shape. Jim was telling me that he thought I had won it. I was low in carbs but had still managed to look pretty good, so was now excited at the prospect of winning another national championship. It wasn't until a guy who looked like Stretch Armstrong walked in that I knew there was going to be a showdown. The contest went as I expected, with me and the big guy going head-to-head. I thought I had it won because my shape and condition was much better, and because of my narrow waist my legs and back would appear bigger than his. The call outs seemed never-ending but this being a Big Guy Federation, the big guy won, beating me by a whisker.

The drive home from the show was even scarier than the drive there, as it was now dark and I was very hungry and very tired. I made sure I was behind the wheel, but this would prove to be near fatal as, at one point, when told to turn right at a roundabout I just turned right, heading into the oncoming traffic, not going round the roundabout at all, then having to swerve around, hitting the central island as I went. Despite the wrong turns and bad driving we managed a much quicker journey home, and more importantly made it home in one piece. This would be the last time I ever drove myself to a show, with the thoughts of Dumb and Dumber springing to mind.

When Monday came it was business as usual, with another three weeks of hitting it hard, up until the British final men's height class 3, 2005. Training was going well, but over the past couple of weeks my favourite cardio bike had opened up a nice deep cut at the top of my leg, which had unfortunately become infected. I knew that the seat had been cutting into me but just thought it was a case of training through the pain, and didn't think too much about it, while all the time I was opening up the same cut day-in, day-out. Bacteria as well as other crap was going into the cut. Before long I was limping about in pain. Eventually I started using a different cycle for my cardio, and within four to five days the pain started to subside, but unfortunately for me the infection had spread, now shifting up into my shoulder and arm. I didn't connect the two at first, assuming it was a separate injury. The infection felt like poison passing through my veins, training was total agony and every now and then I would end up shrieking while working out, as the pain would sometimes be excruciating.

By the next week my arm had doubled in size but then it started to shrink, leaving a dark redness to the whole of the arm, and taking away every grain of detail my arm had. I began to worry, and started showing people in the hope that they would have some idea as to what was causing it or perhaps have some insight as to how to get rid of it. No one seemed to have any answers, and it wasn't until I went to see my friend Bryan Goddard that I would be put right, finally being told what it was. On showing Bryan my arm he immediately became concerned, he started asking me about my symptoms and how it had come about. I told him what had happened. He said it looked like the early stages of septicaemia and that I would have to have it looked at right away. He made a phone call immediately. At this point it all seemed a bit over the top, and I asked Bryan if I could sort it out another day as I was due a meal and wanted to get home. Bryan quickly explained to me that within a few days I could lose my arm completely, in fact with how bad I had already allowed it to get I could potentially lose my life! I said to Bryan "I'll still be able to compete, won't I?" Bryan just looked at me as if to say, I've just told you that you could die and you're talking about competing! Faced with Bryan's scowl, I thought I'd best do as I was told for now.

Bryan had made the call to a guy they called Big Stu. Stu Cosgrove was a well-known physiotherapist, as well as former training partner to bodybuilding legend Dorian Yates, he was also in the Guinness Book of Records as a record-breaking strong man. Stu booked me in as an emergency, and went straight to work on me as

> *I've just told you that you could die*

soon as I arrived. He was trying to massage all the toxins and poisons out of my arm to stop them clogging in one place. He told me that I had been lucky, as my lymph glands had been able to break down the initial infection, but because of the severity of it, the infection had re-formed further up my body. Stu said I needed some strong antibiotics, and showed me various ways of massaging the infection, giving me helpful tips on how to keep breaking it down. He seemed worried, and very anxious to make sure I kept up with what he had said, so when again I asked whether I would be able to compete he told me that competing should be the last thing on my mind.

On the drive home I was thinking about what both Bryan and Stuart had told me. I knew that they knew best; they had been world-class competitors themselves so only had my safety in mind... but still, with all the hard work I had already put in, my only interest was to get onto that stage and compete. Death would have to wait.

One week later, I was still struggling throughout the workouts but was following everything Stuart had told me to the letter. I had just got the prescription for my antibiotics, and started to take them, but with only a week until the contest, my arm was still feeling painful and showing little definition. The couple of days before the contest would be a race to get right that would prove to be a nightmare. I started frantically rubbing my shoulder, trying to get the detail back, but I rubbed so hard and for so long that I took the skin off, making a nice looking scar on my shoulder to add to everything else. I had been carbing-up, throwing around 30 potatoes a day down my neck which was the norm just before a show, but it wasn't the norm to be taking this type of antibiotic at the same time. One of the main side-effects of the antibiotic was mass diarrhoea, so now I was spending as much time on the toilet as I was eating.

My backside was screaming, with the whole house now smelling like shit. It really was a travesty, and would only feel worth it when, the Saturday before the show, I could see the condition of the muscle had somehow returned, with the feeling of poisonous blood vessels now starting to ease. The only thing wrong with me now was my state of mind; I had ignored two of the most knowledgeable gurus in bodybuilding, and even worse had put bodybuilding before life and death.

On the day of the contest (British Championships, men's medium height class, 2005) I was only three pounds heavier than I had been the year earlier, but I was sharper, especially in the legs, so looked more complete overall. Once inside the venue, me and Jim disappeared into the disabled toilets, quickly locking the door. I liked being out of the way come contest day so would usually make the disabled toilet my VIP changing room. Because of my paranoia I also liked being close to a mirror, so would be constantly checking body parts to make sure they were tight as well as seeking reassurance from the person who was with me as to how I looked. Due to my reputation in the sport I would no longer tell many people when I was planning to compete, as I had become afraid of failure, frightened of not being as good as people perceived me to be. I knew there was always a good turnout at the local shows, but I would try to avoid knowing who was there, staying in the shadows until the show had begun.

I had become afraid of failure, frightened of not being as good as people perceived me to be

The contest went off with a bang; Jim had come in looking fantastic and took the title in the over-50s section. Back on stage and pumped myself, I was feeling confident too. The final three were a mixed bag of various shapes and sizes ruling the stage. I thought I had it won, as overall I had the most complete package, with the best overall condition, with my routine going down a storm, with even people I didn't know cheering. The final scores came in and unfortunately I had come in third. I was as gutted as ever, but hearing the boos and hisses coming from the audience, I knew that the crowd had judged it differently, having me as their uncrowned champion. It wasn't everything I would have wanted but it was better than nothing, I knew the contest had been close despite the final result.

The weekend passed, and on the Tuesday I got a call saying the two lads who had placed ahead of me wouldn't be going to the Universe, did I want their spot? The answer of course was "Yes," which meant I was now training for two world titles within a couple of months of each other, the first one only weeks away, the second at the start of the coming year. I was now starting to feel like an international athlete. Jim was really happy I was going; he had arranged for the local paper to come to the gym to take our pictures. I said to Jim that he should be the only focus, as he was the one who had won the titles, but Jim, being his gracious self, would have none of it, and said that having me on the photo would mean a lot to him. Us two competing together would be a fond memory for him, he wanted the picture as something to remember it by. I thought this was a really nice gesture.

me and Jim couldn't work out how to tie our shoelaces

The Mr Universe contest came round and from the get-go things didn't seem to be going to plan. The flight was two hours late getting off the ground, then a crazy taxi ride to the hotel, although in all fairness I slept through most of it. Arriving at the hotel, we were told that none of our suitcases had turned up. As everyone else was tanning up and relaxing, we were making calls and having to mess about. I say we, but should really just say the girls, as me and Jim couldn't work out how to tie our shoelaces at this point, let alone anything else. After several hours we were told our bags were on the way so we could now try and relax a little and get some sleep before the day ahead. The morning travel to the show went smoothly; on getting inside the venue and looking around you could see the standard was good but it was the women that really stood out.

I had heard stories about big German women, now I could see they were true. When first entering the backstage area I saw the biggest woman I had ever seen, she was around six feet tall and must have had around 19-inch ripped arms, with legs to match. Me and Jim thought about having our picture taken with her, but the thought of a woman looking so much bigger than us was more than our egos could take, so we decided to leave it.

A little bit later I was looking for the toilet, I saw what appeared to be a guy going into the jon, so I just followed behind, not looking to see if there was a male or female sign above the door. As I walked in, looking for the stalls, a huge guy with a bald head appeared behind me and at that moment I realised that what I thought was a guy was actually a girl! And the big fella now glaring at me was her boyfriend, I think he thought I was about to get it on with his he/she girlfriend. I looked the room up and down to try to show the guy I had made a mistake by going in the wrong jon, but soon thought, fuck this, and legged it out past him as fast as I could. I had to resort to taking a piss in a plastic bottle behind the door, mint.

I had heard stories about big German women...

It was now time to go on stage, with Jim up first. This was Jim's first international outing so he made the most of it, he looked totally caught up in the moment. He loved every second of the experience but unfortunately his line-up had around 40 or so entrants in it, so he didn't really get seen. It didn't dampen his spirits in any way, it was just one of those things.

When my turn came I knew I wasn't as heavy or quite as sharp as I had been at the British, so I didn't think I would get a look in. My time on stage was similar to what it had been the previous year where I had been compared with the middle of the field, and again like last year, I failed to make the final six. With neither myself nor Jim making the final cut, we decided to have an early night as we had to be up and on our way early the next morning.

The next day would soon come around, with our coach arriving before we even had a chance to have any breakfast, then from the coach there was a long train journey into Cologne. It was the first time in months that I could eat what I wanted but I still hadn't had anything since teatime the day before. When we arrived at the station we realised there wasn't much to do, and as we would have to stay there until the middle of the afternoon we decided to have a walk outside. We could see a cathedral so thought we'd go in, just to pass a little time. When we had finished looking around we were thinking about going back, but before heading back we noticed a few market stalls and could hear something going on. We got round the corner and to our surprise we discovered the Cologne outdoor winter market. Right away you could smell the food cooking on what had been a cold morning. The place was picture perfect, this would be the first time I had sensed the smell of Christmas. Soon I was tucking in to everything I could get my teeth into, with it turning out to be a great memorable winter's day, I couldn't have picked a better place to come off my diet.

> *I kept saying I needed to sit down, she kept saying we were nearly there*

On the way home things weren't so good as I had become overly tired. Christina took charge, running us ragged trying to get us to our terminal so we could make the plane in time. I kept saying I needed to sit down, she kept saying we were nearly there, but at this point I was seeing black dots, and as we reached the back of the line I lost consciousness, ending up collapsing in the queue. When I came round I was on the floor, Jim was arguing with some guy, trying to get his bottle of water for me to drink. It was the first time I had ever seen Jim lose his rag. I was OK this time, but it was an upsetting end to an already tough year... and within eight weeks I would have to do it all again.

On getting back it was only a matter of days until I was back training. I had decided that up to Christmas I would keep my carbs moderate, and try to get a balance with enough carbs to keep fuller and stronger, but not enough to make me put on weight then not be able to keep my condition. Following Christmas I planned to drop back then diet down for the show. The first couple of weeks were hard to gauge, as the bounce-back and sudden insulin surge of eating the extra carbs left me looking smooth and, in some places, bloated. I decided to stick with my plan, but come Christmas I still couldn't gauge what was fat and what was water retention, so over the festive period there would be no drinks or pudding, I even vetted the Christmas dinner, having mainly just vegetables and turkey. Christina and I still had fun. We would get wrapped up and go for long walks, stopping off at the odd tavern where Christina could enjoy a well-deserved glass of wine, while I supped a black coffee with a bottle of water to go. Despite the diet and the training, Christmas still remained the special occasion it had always been.

IT WAS AN UPSETTING END TO AN ALREADY TOUGH YEAR... AND WITHIN EIGHT WEEKS I WOULD HAVE TO DO IT ALL AGAIN.

CHAPTER 18

My first breakthrough, becoming world class

It was the start of 2006, and now that the water retention and any blur on my physique had gone, I was able to see exactly what I had to do to get myself right for the coming Mr Universe contest. The answer turned out to be to do nothing! My physique was in great shape, way fuller than ever before. Even though I was heavier, I had more vascularity and separation, with the added calories giving my physique a much fresher look. I now realised that I hadn't really seen my physique at its best the year earlier, due to all the injuries and setbacks I had suffered. I carried on with what I was doing and decided to use common sense over science, just keeping an eye on the progression as I went. I would only drop back on my carbs around three weeks before the show, and only for ten days, then I would carb back up until two days before the contest. This wasn't the usual technique, I used only impulse to guide me on this one, I knew it would be as much about luck as about judgment.

It was another flight, but this time only Christina and I were making the trip. The flight went well with the morning after going by quickly, then after an early breakfast and a brief coach trip we were at the venue and ready to take on the day. It was hard to find a decent space backstage as it looked massively over-cluttered. Luckily we found a spot right behind the door, then made a little barricade with chairs and bags in order to have our own space. Even better, there was a mirror on the back of the door so I could keep my paranoia about how I was looking to a limit, so would feel a little more at ease. Christina went through the ritual backstage drill of getting me tanned up while constantly telling me I was looking good, before shooting off, getting to the front of the stage to take photos when my class came on. She did all this, as well as being my one-woman audience and cheering me on as I came on stage; and there's me thinking I had it tough.

The time came for my class to be called, all the competitors were lined up behind the curtain waiting, pumping up, taking our last glances in the mirror before we went on. As we all stood looking in the mirror I could see just how much better I had been than the previous year, and for the first time while hitting my poses I felt flawless in how I looked. Even though some of the guys were bigger, and I knew I wasn't going to win, there was no one there that I would rather have looked like than me. My lifetime dream of how I had always wanted to look had finally come to pass, and I felt like a champion even before setting foot on stage. Would the judges be as impressed by me as I was?

Would the judges be as impressed by me as I was?

After the first three or four call-outs I was starting to get seen. But this time I felt I was being called out with the better competitors, and that I had come back into the competition a little more than usual. Still, when I came off stage, I couldn't be sure if it had been good enough to make the final six. Now backstage, it wasn't long before the guy with the clipboard came around to announce the final six from our class. I was more anxious than ever, and stood right next to him as he started reading out the names. He had got to the fourth name and still nothing, my fear of failure was starting to kick in, my arse now twitching. Then he got to the fifth name, and it was me. I broke into an American-style frenzy, yelling "Woooooo-hoooooo!" like I was a nut-job. The other competitors were smiling and shaking my hand, seeing just how much this final placing had obviously meant to me.

> *I broke into an American-style frenzy, yelling "Woooooo-hoooooo!" like I was a nut-job.*

After I had got myself together and got dressed, Christina came running in to me, I told her the news. She started telling me about a guy she had spoken to while I was competing, a magazine photographer. She had pointed me out, so he had started taking a load of shots of me whilst I'd been on stage. I got my stuff together, then we both set off to speak to the guy. When we arrived at the front Christina was welcomed into the officials section, but I had to wait outside the rope. It turned out that being a small good-looking blonde had more pull than being an official world-competitor. Luckily I did find this quite funny as she trundled past me, laughing.

She soon brought the photographer over, then we all sat as he opened up his laptop. When he showed me the pictures he had taken I was in disbelief, I could see I was every bit as good as I thought I had been. I was now more over the moon than ever, as not only had I made the final six, and was looking the best I'd ever been, but it had all been caught on camera as well. The day at this point couldn't have gone any better. When the night show came around my run of luck ran short, with sixth being my final placing, but if you'd seen my face and reactions, you would have sworn I had just won. As I left the stage I was shaking everyone's hand as well as throwing out a few extra poses as I went. This was my greatest international glory to date, I had placed in the final six elite. I had weighed in at 13 stone five pounds, which was my heaviest stage weight, as well as appearing in my finest condition. Now with my early 2006 season success I could enjoy a good off-season with a view to coming back in the mid-season of 2007 with a bang.

Back home and back down the gym, young Alex had been on my case for quite a while, constantly trying to sneak into my workouts. I had told him of young training partners gone by, about how I had been let down by them, and that I wasn't looking to get close with anyone and would prefer to train alone. But Alex kept turning up, knowing what time I trained, joining in regardless, always asking advice about developing different body parts as well as other stuff. I had never met anyone as persistent as he was, so after a while I knew I would have to either report him for being a stalker or make him my new training partner. In the end I went with the latter choice.

At the start things were a little sketchy, I was on Alex's case with how he was spotting, particularly when he kept dripping sweat in my eyes and mouth while spotting me on the bench press. What would make matters worse was when I was shouting at Alex the likes of Andy Mc, Ste, Harry and Big Phil started shouting stuff like "Lovers' tiff!" and "Do you want to borrow my headband?", making me even more frustrated. Alex would eventually start bringing a towel for his sweaty head, and after a while we started using dumbbells rather than the bar, so with this Alex's spotting and enthusiasm would soon be second to none. Every workout we had was better than the last, and with no mid-season contests to worry about we could really hit the off-season hard. Alex was growing at a rate I'd never seen before, with me also reaching my heaviest, notching up around 16 and a half stone.

There was one night when we were training after hours, there was a power cut. It was leg night, but the gym was in total darkness. We decided to train using only the lights from our mobile phones to guide the way. As we loaded up the bar, then set ourselves up for the squat, the light from the phones kept going off, leaving us squatting what I think was about 240kg in total darkness. It was a workout

Hercules would have been proud of, and couldn't have looked more fitting if it had in fact taken place on Mount Olympus itself. This would be the most near perfect training year I had ever had. Power cuts, earthquakes, lightning, nothing was going to stop us.

POWER CUTS, EARTHQUAKES, LIGHTNING, NOTHING WAS GOING TO STOP US.

CHAPTER 19

Love and loss

In my personal life, myself and Christina had also enjoyed a good year, we were talking about having children. The setting in which we lived was nice, very family oriented, and friendships with our neighbours couldn't have been any better, so we thought it was now time to start our own little family. This was what Christina had wanted for a while; I had put it off, but now I thought the time was right and a child in our lives would be a good thing.

I wanted a boy, and Christina a girl, and before Christina had even hit pregnancy we were talking about names, what our child might look like, who they would take after, with the excitement of family life being regularly brought up in our daily conversations. After a couple of months of trying, Christina got a positive result on her pregnancy test, and with how she looked at me you would have thought that all her Christmases had come at once, it was an exciting time. Within weeks we were telling everyone the good news and they looked over the moon as we told them. Christina couldn't stop herself from buying things. One day, when we had gone for a walk around the lake, she glimpsed a baby boutique which was set amongst a small row of quaint little shops. Once inside she spotted this tiny little pink coat, and already having presumed we were having a little girl, she had to buy it. Around 12 weeks went by, by which time Christina was in full bloom, she had started to get that radiant healthy look pregnant women sometimes get. She seemed so happy, now both of us were looking forward to the first scan, seeing what our little baby would look like at this early stage in pregnancy.

Everyone was wishing us luck, the thought of having this child had become very much a reality to us both. We were even at the stage where we were messing about, talking to the baby through the stomach, looking at cots and buggies, debating what colour the nursery was going to be. It had all been a lot of fun. We were now at the hospital waiting to be scanned. The lady carrying out the scan spoke pleasantly with Christina as they were friends, and had worked together at some point in the past. The lady was now holding the scanner looking to see the baby. "Here we are," she pleasantly said, whilst showing us the image of our baby on the screen. We were grinning, waiting to see our child's first movements. She then said, "Just give it a second," as she moved the scanner round, trying different angles, various attempts were made, but in the end, and after a very long awkward silence, she had to tell us that our child had no heartbeat and had died. As I viewed what I now knew was the corpse of what would have been our first child, I felt a feeling of hurt that had been unknown to me up until now. It felt like someone had hit me in the middle of the head with a wooden bat. Now forcing back the tears and breathing heavily I was looking at Christina who had the most haunted look I had ever seen. Although able to hold her, I was unable to say any words that might help, I just wanted us to leave the hospital as quickly as possible. On getting home things were tough, when telling my mum she started ranting, saying "Oh, no! No!" with tears running down her face.

Having to spread the word was hard, and knowing people truly felt for us made things even worse. I had to console Christina endlessly over the first few weeks as this child to her had truly become a reality, with her already very much in love with it. On the surface I would seem OK, and in work, like down the gym, I could get on with things, looking like nothing bothered me. Even when at home I would be positive when talking to Christina, already talking about trying again and not giving up, but there would be one instant when, alone, I caught a glimpse of the little pink coat

Christina and I had bought at the lake and right away my mind went back to that day and how happy we had both been. I locked myself away, still sat looking at the coat, now letting go with tears and loud shrieks. Finally, I was coming to terms with things.

In the coming weeks things started to improve and when out on my round I started trying to move my mind to next year's competitive season. This is what I always did when I had a lot on my mind, I would make notes of what I would be doing, how much I would be weighing and at what point, starting to form a plan of which shows I would want to do. I wrote out my plans in the night-time, putting everything down as well as reading endless amounts of nutrition journals. My mind was still swaying back and forth, but now at least I was starting to look forward, trying to remain positive with my bodybuilding as well as holding on to the idea that we could try again for a family in the near future.

I knew there was no future in the past

Luckily it wouldn't be long until Christina would get caught again and for a short while all would be well – but after only around three or four weeks this time Christina suffered an even earlier miscarriage.

She still hadn't recovered from the first one, so when not at work was bedbound a lot of the time. She wanted to point fingers, mowing over the past, her emotions starting to get the better of her. I knew there was no future in the past, so would have to draw a line, calling off our bid to start a family at this time, treating it like a failed project, cutting out the human element to it altogether. Life had been good for a while with this being the only setback; I thought it best to put it behind us, so when Christina started talking about the miscarriage, or trying again, I kept brushing it off until she got the message, and eventually she stopped bringing it up. Although this seemed cold-hearted, this way of doing things would eventually work, with the past upset slowly but surely fading into the background. In the latter end of 2006 we would be back as we once were, but with no talk of babies entering the conversation.

My plans for the coming season were all laid out. I was looking forward to next year's challenge and had decided on doing the double, aiming to win both the Men's weight class British, and also the Men's height class British, both in the same year. Winning them both would put me in the big league, as well as being a good safeguard into the international scene, which I was now aiming for. I knew it was going to be a long year as I would be starting my diet from the beginning of February and going right through until November, this would be the longest time I had ever dieted. This was the cleverest diet and exercise plan I had ever thought up, aimed to trigger metabolism, as well as keeping my body anti-catabolic without at any point reaching burn-out, or having to be anti-social (well, at least not for the best part of it all anyway).

Before the start of the long-winded diet I thought it might be a good idea to have a short break, so I decided to spend a week away in Philadelphia, the home of the Rocky films. With Rocky Balboa now on the big screen, and the steps from the movie being just up the street from the hotel, it was the perfect place to take a break as well as getting motivated at the same time.

After the trip, I went to work, my plan going off without any kind of glitch or set-back. By the middle of the year I was already in good shape. The plan was perfect and even three months in, my social life hadn't been affected. Even though I wasn't allowing myself any drinks or food I was still attending BBQs in the neighbourhood, as well as enjoying social life with work, going out on organised events more than ever. The banter through the day didn't alter as we would still argue sometimes, whether or not I was training for a show, so it didn't make any noticeable difference at this point.

My married life had been on a high also, but unfortunately through one misunderstanding this was all about to change. A few of us at work had organised an outing, but because one friend was running behind after attending a football match I couldn't pick him up from his home at the time planned. At the same time, one of the girls who was also going on the trip needed a lift so I offered to pick her up on the way into town whilst waiting for my friend to get back. I had told Christina the original plan to meet some friends in Bury, but I hadn't mentioned picking anyone up on the way. I said my goodbyes to Christina, who was soon off herself visiting her sister, and was soon at my friend's house, knocking on the door, but with no answer. I sent him a text to see where he was, he sent one back saying he would call me when he got home. I decided to go and get Julie (my friend from work who needed the lift) while I was waiting. As I arrived, Julie's friend opened the door, saying Julie was still getting ready and for me to come inside. It wasn't long before she was ready, and we all sat in the house having a drink and just waiting for my pal to call, but the next call I got wouldn't be the one I was expecting.

> *the next call I got wouldn't be the one I was expecting*

Christina, on her way up to her sister's, had spotted my car and had pulled up to see why it was there. She had asked a neighbour whose house this was, and was now on the phone asking what I was doing and why was I in Julie's house. For some reason I didn't take it on, I just told the truth, but didn't go out to see her and sort it. I was thinking that she had followed me and was keeping an eye on me. I wasn't up to anything, so I thought why should I be answerable to anyone? I felt annoyed and it made me more determined to go on this trip than ever. I eventually did go out, but by that time Christina was gone, so I decided to carry on the night as planned, and deal with the situation the next day.

The following day Christina was as mad as a hatter, accusing me of all sorts, she was going crackers so I had to leave the house and spent a couple of nights sleeping at the gym. Christina's thoughts on what had happened were running deep, she was thinking the worst. When I went home I spent the better part of the week having to talk her round, as well as having to do some excessive creeping. Eventually we did get things sorted, but I had to show her pictures of the night for her to believe my story and even on seeing them she still wasn't sure, but for now things seemed to go back to normal.

However stressful my home life was, it wouldn't affect my gym. My competition prep was going swimmingly, and going into August I was enjoying the whole experience, basking in the cleverness of my contest plan. I was getting to the stage where I had started going into myself a little, and was opting out of most chat and socialising. I had started developing a strange obsession with doing my cardio in the early hours of the morning in order not to have to speak to anyone; the scary thing was, I was loving it. I had stuck very close to my original plan, with the only thing changing being that rather than just forming a plan to cover my waking hours, I would start to use the full 24 hours in the day. A lot of the time in the middle of the night I used to wake up, lying there doing nothing, then the next day I would find myself feeling tired, less attentive and eager, while doing my training and cardio. Now I would change all that, and after waking, regardless of the time, I would just get up, black coffee, then go out power walking for an hour or sometimes more. It was pitch-black most the time, but the fresh morning air would feel inviting.

I would regularly visit the nearby cemetery

I would regularly visit the nearby cemetery, walking down the river's edge to get there. The places that scared most people became the places I would love the most; the darkness, and the fact that no one at all would be around, would add to the whole experience. I enjoyed being in the graveyard just as the sky was starting to turn blue, with the birds starting to sing their morning songs. My mind would be at ease, with my thoughts positive and carefree. My normally boring cardio now became my favourite part of the day. On returning home after being out in the fresh air I would usually grab an hour or so power nap, before waking again, then getting ready for work.

Myself and Alex were still training together most the time, both of us coming into shape. I would think of Alex when at my most tired and vulnerable. As I had given him the speeches about keeping with the plan, and not giving up, I had to make sure I stuck to what I said. I had to walk the walk, not just talk the talk. I couldn't think of anything worse than someone preaching about what to do then not being able to do it themselves.

While in the gym, now working up to the contest, it felt similar to how it was back when I was training with Rob, with people hanging around watching us train, wanting our time, believing everything we said to them. One of my favourite examples of this was when I had cut my arm whilst on the cable crossovers, then just carried on training as if nothing was wrong. A young kid came up and asked why my arm was bleeding. I replied, in a cheesy heroic type manner, that sometimes when you train so hard, you sweat blood. The kid just looked in awe, then asked "Really?" in total belief. I started to laugh, shaking my head before carrying on with my next set. The kid had looked so impressed that I didn't have the heart to tell him any different.

when I talked about winning the double, most people seemed to expect nothing less

The most notable difference, when talking about belief, was that only a few years earlier, when I talked to other people about the shows I hoped to win, a lot of them had been sceptical, but now when I talked about winning the double, most people seemed to expect nothing less. I was now being perceived the way I had always wanted to be.

Another outing at work had been organised and even though I was tired and a little less social, I decided to go on it. It was the annual dog-racing trip, which was always popular; this one no different with everyone in good spirits, and the added bonus of good weather to top it off. It turned out to be a great day, which was good, as it would be my last day out now until after contest time. Although I was smartly dressed, both my pockets had sweet potato and turkey lodged in them, for when it was meal time. This had been the norm for me for many years when on outings.

Christina had been texting me throughout the day, but I had been unable to get back to her as my phone had no service from where I was, so I just presumed that I would speak to her as normal when I got back, I didn't see it as a problem. On my return home Christina started kicking off about the fact that I hadn't texted her, and even with me trying to explain, she was just firing off at me without any real explanation. It wasn't long before Julie's name was brought up, with the events of last time coming into play. She was still upset about the last outing, and this was just the start of things to come. She had also been going through my phone and had misinterpreted certain texts that had gone on between myself and Julie, amongst others. It wasn't long before the argument had reached fever pitch. I was about to lose my temper, but instead, I quickly left the house

I spent the best part of the night walking round aimlessly, eventually coming back in the early hours, then retreating to the spare room. In the next week or so nothing changed, and in between the arguments there were long drawn-out silences, with Christina constantly asking me to leave the house at random intervals. I tried to ignore her, carrying on with my prep like there was nothing wrong, but one night she did manage to get under my skin, forcing me to lose my temper, I was throwing things, ranting, generally going fucking nuts, still not knowing why she was being this way. Before long the police had arrived, as Christina had called them whilst I was having my frenzy. I was taken away, not able to return for the next couple of days or when allowed by the police.

This had all been an absolute nightmare, yet even though I sensed my marriage was on the scrapheap, all I could think about was the contest, and how hard I had worked and prepared for it. Never once did I stop to think about how Christina was, nor was I thinking about putting it right. I had very little human emotion, with my only logic while going through all this being that I knew I hadn't cheated, so why should I have to sort anything out? I couldn't believe how out of control it all was, but I still wasn't willing to take it on. I moved back up to my mum and dad's, offering them little more than a brief explanation, and started my contest preparation right away. I had finished work, as I always booked my leave around my contests. Apart from my morning aerobics and gym-time there was little else to worry about, and not having to see or speak to anyone made life even better. My mum, dad and sister Debra never delved into what was going on, they knew what my bodybuilding meant to me, so there was never anything brought up about my home life, they never once bothered me, which was always appreciated.

Never once did I stop to think about how Christina was

I didn't have to plan a new path for my morning aerobics, as the walk I had done from being a boy was right outside my door. The obsession with the early mornings hadn't gone away, I was still up in the early hours, heading for the hills, with my morning coffee, almost excited about the dark path ahead. There was one morning when walking up the old road I saw a mist appear all around, but it only rose to around waist high. When I got as far as the old church I was excited by what looked like a scene from an old vampire movie, with all the gravestones swamped in mist apart from the tops. I wandered around the graves and the old church, captivated by the scene. I can honestly say I didn't want the morning to end, but knew it would, as the sky was already starting to come light, so also like a vampire, when the blue skies appeared I would disappear.

There would be the odd occasion when I bumped into someone I knew while out walking in the dark, they might be going to work or doing the night security shift. I used to think I would have to explain myself, but when we got talking they would usually have smiles on their faces, already knowing why I was there, and for some reason they would be easy about it. I found it funny that my obvious weirdness was so easily accepted by the people who knew me, they were fascinated by my strange dedication, often telling their friends about me.

On the other hand, there would be the odd early morning dog walker who would catch a glimpse of me and quickly grab their dog and leg it off in the other direction. It was all good. The dark mornings would be my comfort – which in itself tells you just how far from the real world I had ventured. When talking to people at this point, anything to do with relationships, gossip, or even just general chit-chat would have no interest to me, and often when people would go on with themselves I couldn't feel any empathy toward their problems. I would just be hoping that they would go away, as in most cases I didn't know what they were talking about! All I was thinking about was my next meal or if my abs were looking any tighter.

British championships 2007, under 85kg. All the crew was there. There was my sister Deb and my good friend and on/off training partner Andy Whittle, as well as my current training partner and apprentice Alex Clarke. We were sitting in the house and I was making sure I had all my bits together, just going through the list, when I heard the letterbox clang. I went to get the mail, noticing a large A4 envelope on top of the pile with my name on it. At first I thought it was just the poster or an invite for my next show, but as I opened it I could tell it was an official letter. Christina had filed for divorce, with the papers appearing the morning of the show. I had been unaffected with it all up until now, but knowing what the letter was about I instantly sank, my heart beating heavily. I felt an instant unpleasantness, which is hard to describe; only people who have been there themselves will know what I mean. I didn't make a secret of what it was, I knew from how everyone looked that they already knew something was wrong. I just said the words "Divorce papers" before turning to go upstairs, heading towards the bathroom.

I was staring at myself in the mirror, doing my best to stay calm, trying to control my breathing. I was chanting words under my breath about not being beat, not being kept down, being able to walk through walls. I did this in order to get re-psyched, so that on going downstairs I could appear like nothing bothered me, looking positive like I had done only minutes before receiving the letter.

I JUST SAID THE WORDS DIVORCE PAPERS BEFORE TURNING TO GO UPSTAIRS, HEADING TOWARDS THE BATHROOM.

I sensed for the first time a dark horizon

CHAPTER 20

Back to back British titles focus overpowering loss

On the journey down, I had a lot on my mind. The worry of not winning was at the forefront of it. I sensed for the first time a dark horizon in my near future; I knew that not winning the contests, as well as losing my marriage, would definitely be enough to take me down. Even a winning streak wouldn't be enough to get me out of this jam, but it might just be enough to keep my head right long enough to get over what I was about to go through with the divorce.

By the time we had reached the show venue I'd managed to rekindle my belief that when the shows were over I could still put things right at home, with all not lost just yet. If there was anything I was good at it was getting myself back into a positive mind-set, dealing with the immediate tasks ahead. As we all arrived at the venue, that's exactly what I had to do.

I stood in line, waiting to weigh in. The day earlier I had weighed in around 86kg, but I knew after dropping my water I would be down to around 84kg, which would put me a kilo under the needed weight, which was about right. When it was my turn to get on the scales, I thought they were wrong as I was just under 81kg which didn't seem possible, but on stepping on the scales once more, I had to accept that they were right. I had lost water from within the muscle, not just the surface water I had wanted to lose. My positivity levels began to drop, I was desperate to find a mirror to see where the weight had gone from, praying that it wasn't from my legs or shoulders.

When the time came to be called backstage, myself and Alex were first in there and within minutes of finding a spot to get set up, I had my pants around my ankles to see how my legs were looking. It was a good start, my legs looked better than ever, they had a fuller shape with thick separation right through. I felt better. Taking my shirt off, again I looked shredded; even though my upper body didn't look as full as it had done, it was still very sharp and luckily hadn't flattened out. It looked like most of the water had been taken from my back and waistline, which were the two best places it could have come from. Before long all the competitors were in the mirror, eying each other up, figuring out who was the best. I knew a few of the favourites in the contest, with the two most talked about being a former European Champion and the former Junior British Champion; but knew I was in there and that it was going to be a good contest.

When out on stage the judging didn't seem to be taking much direction with there seeming to be a lot of odd call-outs, leaving me none the wiser as to who had placed where. I wanted to get a feel for how I had done. Whilst getting ready I got talking to Nigel (the lad who I had done my first Mr Universe with, a couple of years earlier) and he said he thought I deserved the victory, but then also commented on how political the show had been, and how the young former Junior Champion had been plugged to win in my class. I wished I hadn't spoken to him, my mind was on overtime right up until getting back on stage for the night show, just hoping it was going to be a fair result.

Although the day had taken its time it eventually came to the final round up, the final five taking their places for the countdown. The former European Champion somehow finished fifth; I thought he may have just pinched it as his shots from the rear were outstanding, but the judges must have seen something different.

The countdown carried on, with some of the more deserving competitors stopping one or two spots short of the placings I thought they deserved. When it came down to the final two I started to doubt the outcome, thinking Nigel's words may have been right, as there was just me and the former Junior now standing for the final result. It took what felt like an eternity, but when I heard the announcement for second place, and it wasn't me, I knew I had done it, once more I was champion. I felt both joy and massive relief, with my main aim now met. Even with all the odds against me I had managed to live up to what I had set out to do. I'd never felt more relieved in all my life. As I got backstage I was greeted by Andy and Debra, and for some reason we found ourselves standing together, looking into the mirror, all of us starry-eyed. They had both wanted this victory for me as much as I had wanted it for myself. It was one of those moments, a moment that for some reason would never leave me.

The night wasn't quite over. I knew that in order to get into the international scene with this Federation I would have to place in the final three overall, something that I hadn't managed to do in the past. The final pose-down came, with me getting several call-outs amongst the final three, so I knew it was close. When the results came, I hadn't quite won the overall but had come a close second, and with this I knew I would have my pick of shows within the international sector of the Federation. I could leave the show a happy man, hopeful that next year, international notoriety would be on its way.

I WOULD HAVE MY
PICK OF SHOWS

I put the phone down
knowing my marriage
was over.

CHAPTER 21

Breaking up, breaking down

The next couple of weeks went by without a hitch and for the second British final I was right on the money, this time weighing in at 13 stone, six pounds, my heaviest stage weight so far. British championship, 2007, men's height class 3. This was a local show so would always bring a good crowd and a good atmosphere with it. Again I brought home the bacon by winning my second British title in two weeks; winning the double like I had intended. In the overall it would be the three shorter class winners going up against one another, and three taller classes, with the winner of each coming together to decide the champion of champions on the evening. I did pretty well by winning amongst the three short classes, but was unable to fend off the larger heavyweight for the final overall placing. It didn't matter, I had achieved what I had intended, job done.

The night after the show, myself and Alex grabbed a well-deserved pizza and talked about our bodybuilding futures. Alex had enjoyed a good year, bagging both the English and UK under-18s titles – he now looked destined for better things. Well-known gurus in the sport were offering their advice, wanting to take him under their wing, which I was glad of to a point as I had helped him get this far but also wanted him to reach the next level.

Alex was very career-orientated for such a young lad, he knew what he wanted and would stop at nothing to get it. He had already told me that this would be the last year I would help mentor him, but he was thankful for the knowledge and time I had spent with him, we would still be good friends even though parting company. I was happy with this as in the past I had helped several youngsters, with most either turning on me when they realised they weren't like me and couldn't do what I did, or just not bothering, letting me down without a thought when they couldn't reach the goals they had set for themselves. Alex had been dedicated, sticking with me for nearly three years in order to learn his craft. He had proved his worth by winning everything possible in his age bracket, and I was glad to have assisted, being a big part of his early progression.

The next week, the local newspaper got in touch, wanting my picture and story. At first I thought I would have the picture with me winning the two British titles as the main focus, but then I thought I would bring Alex in as well, then we could share the picture, giving Alex his first taste of media exposure. Now the story would be about two training partners bagging four national titles, this had not been done before in the history of our town. The latter end of the story would be about me and my venture into international competition.

This year I appeared in several bodybuilding magazines, getting great write-ups, taking centre-stage in a lot of the pictures. I was at the top of my game, having won five national titles, four of them being British finals. I had three international appearances, with one them being a final six placing, and my sights were firmly set on winning the Mr Universe title. From this point until the end of my career I would only compete internationally, at either European or world championships. I would vary Federations, weights, heights, in accordance to how I wanted my physique to look. I would never take much note of where I was travelling to, it was always just about winning the shows, never sightseeing. In most cases I would barely leave my room when competing internationally, with the plane journeys being more a hindrance than anything else. I was already in training for the year ahead without even as much as a couple of days' rest following my two title victories.

I had wanted to take a training vacation for some time now, with hopes of visiting California, but somehow whilst pursuing this, I would get talking to Christina. For the first time since breaking up she wanted to try and sort things out. I initially thought to get it sorted when I got back, but when thinking it through, and knowing I hadn't given an inch whilst competing, I thought it would show willing if I cancelled my plans, putting my relationship first this time. When not on a diet my mind worked as it should, like it used to. It actually felt good to be considerate again, using emotion rather than just cold-blooded moral logic, but unlike previous years that had panned out well by Christmas, this time I wasn't going to be so lucky. Within a week or so, we were back at each other's throats, with the fights and fallouts reaching new levels. With no resolve we would once again have to go our separate ways.

This year I had taken on a second job, working in a children's home for the mentally challenged, as well as for kids who had gone off the rails. Looking for extra shifts to fill my time, I was also looking for door work, just anything to get me out so I wasn't stuck in come the weekend. I was now fully aware that my marriage could well and truly be over, starting to feel the hurt I had dreaded now creeping in. Even with the support of family and friends all wanting to get me out or include me in their get-togethers, I was struggling to come to terms with losing Christina, finding myself making excuses not to go out. Even while attending a couple of outings I felt alone, regardless of how many people came over to speak with me. It felt like when you read one of those love novels, or watch a romantic movie, and they are going on about a part of them being missing when they are no longer with the one they love. It turns out that shit is actually true, because that's exactly how I felt. I didn't at any point burst into tears but I was constantly lost. I was frantically trying to fill my time the best I could, something I had always done when the chips were down.

It didn't take me long to find some work on the door, getting myself a spot working a club in a nearby town. When I first returned it seemed like a blessing, but unfortunately the blessing wouldn't last. There was a glass collector who wanted to become a doorman at the place I worked, he had just got his badge. He wanted the position I had, but instead of just waiting for a post to come up he thought that if he bullied me, I would leave. For the first couple of weeks the guy was constantly giving me shit, walking into me, talking down to me whenever he had the chance. Finally, at the end of a pretty shit shift he decided to try it on, and got right into my face, actually hitting me with his head this time, but this time he had pushed it too far, flipping my switch from cool to boiling, forcing me to react. I grabbed the lad's face then smashed his head off the wall a couple of times, leaving him dumbfounded against one of the chairs. Later in the week I received a call – the guy had said I was the bully, that he couldn't work if I was there, and that he was pressing charges. So that was that, my job on the door was gone.

Now I was looking to be out come Saturday night, as the thought of staying in was killing me, especially with it being so close to Christmas. I regularly saw my cousin Phil throughout the week, he started getting me out over the Christmas period, making sure I wasn't stuck in, mulling things over. My time was filled with training, work, nights out and spending time with close friends; but despite all this I was still missing my wife.

Come Christmas Day I was at my sister Karen's for dinner, again feeling very much alone within myself, almost ghost-like. I was thinking of Christina, the good times we had shared, smiling to myself almost as if she was there. Soon after, I started to panic, with a sense of sudden urgency, knowing I had to see her. Later that night, when the house was at its loudest with the party in full swing, I sneaked away off through the back, got into my car and headed down to see Christina at our house, thinking she would be in alone, and that if any day was a good day to make up, this was it. As I arrived I could see the house was in blackness, so right away I knew she wasn't home. I went inside and laid out the presents I had bought for her. At the same time I noticed there weren't any there from her to me. I sat for a while, but the house we had shared no longer felt like home, so I locked up and left, driving down the old track next to the river. Against my better judgement I found myself texting Christina, asking where she was. She got back telling me she was at her mum's, asking what I wanted. Not thinking too much I said I had popped down to give her some presents and had just wanted to see how she was. We went back and forth for a while until finally Christina called it a day, reminding me that it was me who had wanted the freedom, she also said that I hadn't addressed anything, or been remotely bothered about the relationship when I was competing, my own words now coming back to haunt me, her final words being that it was time we both moved on. I put the phone down knowing my marriage was over. I stared out into the blackness, angry yet upset at the same time, but I was already thinking about competing in the coming year, looking forward to when my emotions would be cut off. I hoped the care and thought for others wouldn't exist, so that this lonely darkness I was now glaring into would soon become my favourite retreat once more.

2007 had been a good year for me as a bodybuilder, but come the next year there would have to be an even greater success come my way just in order for me to keep my head right, to stop me from sinking. Now bodybuilding would be my way out; it was a need, a necessary addiction. We talk about drug addiction, but any addiction can be lethal, needing that new high but not being able to reach it could easily be enough to bury anyone.

By early 2008 life down the gym was going well, I was more well-regarded and respected than I had ever been. I was a mess inside, but at least for now everything else seemed to be going OK, with a lot of the younger members now wanting my advice which I was more than willing to give. Amongst others there were two young lads that had been constantly keen, for months now pecking my head, asking me for help. I had been training on my own since

Alex had gone his own way, so I thought it time I got myself some new training partners, with these two lads in mind, and if they turned out to be any good perhaps I would have them both train with me up to my next contest. While it was still early in the year I could spend more time showing them correct techniques, good spotting, helping them both with their diets.

The first young lad was called Steve Grimes, I had noted him constantly watching me train, asking odd questions between sets. He was small, well put together, but appeared less than confident in his manner. I could see he was a genuine lad so thought I would give him a chance, I wanted to bring him out of himself a little too. He was looking for direction so when I asked him if he wanted to train with me, he was all over it. It was the first time I had seen him smile or look excited about anything.

The other guy was called John Mark, I had known him a while. He too was well-mannered, even though I'd heard he could be a handful, and had been a local tough-nut whilst growing up. John was quietly confident, but lacked a lot of charisma and drive. He wanted to compete, and even though I was a little unsure of taking on another apprentice, I would agree to help him out. It was a three-man team, which wasn't normally my thing, but I knew that if I could get the workouts speeding along with everyone on board, it could work.

My home life had been somewhat different, I had spent the first couple of months moving in and out of different places, with a lot of the places I lived not very nice. It was Matt who would get me settled eventually. He owned a house but had moved out, so had let me stop there for a while. For the first couple of months I worked on doing the place up, as it hadn't been maintained since he had moved, but the DIY was good for keeping my mind off things. The house was empty, dark and cold when I first started sleeping there but when I'd finished, I'd got it looking like a home. Once Matt saw that I had done the place up and was hoping to stay there a while, he got all the electric and water back on for me so I could live there properly, he even sorted a settee for me so I wouldn't have to sleep on the floor. My mum and dad had been good for letting me stay and hadn't forced me out in any way, but they had made plans to redecorate the bedrooms, plus I didn't like putting on anyone any longer than I had to. Matt's house was just outside the town, far enough away so I wouldn't have to worry about running into my soon-to-be ex-wife too often. During this year, apart from going to work and to the gym, I would spend very little time around my home town.

I wasn't socialising much, the only person I would spend a lot of time with was my cousin Phil who would act as a kind of counsellor whist becoming my closest friend. When I was feeling blue, he would try to get me to see the light, always giving me good and positive advice, doing his best to make sure I was OK. If for any reason I hadn't turned up at his house when I was expected, he would turn up at mine, watching over me like an older brother, precious. I had got my training team, my new out-of-the-way house, and my closest friends there for when I needed them, what could possibly go wrong?

NOW BODYBUILDING WOULD BE MY WAY OUT; IT WAS A NEED, A NECESSARY ADDICTION

whilst compiling the perfect
plan I had missed out the most
important thing

CHAPTER 22

Negativity breeding negativity

When they say negativity breeds negativity they're not far wrong. I had put everything in place for my next competitive season to run smoothly, but whilst compiling the perfect plan I had missed out the most important thing. I hadn't given myself any real time to get over my break up. I just hadn't taken it on, anybody speaking with me wouldn't have known anything was wrong in my home life, only the people I was close with would ever know. As it turned out, it wouldn't take much of a bad thing to turn a positive plan into a negative disaster.

The banter in the gym had always been a little savage, and I don't know if it was my frame of mind but when some of the lads decided it would be fun to take the piss out of my current marital situation I found it very hard to deal with. I tried not to show it at first, which was probably my biggest mistake as within a couple of weeks it became constant, to the point that I was taking it home with me.

The thing I was trying to put behind me was being brought up time and time again, getting me more and more worked up. I was fighting my corner in the banter department, but with the diet kicking in I was running out of things to come back with, as well as running out of patience. The whole thing was now starting to eat me up, I knew it wouldn't be long until I lost it.

The first issue was with one of the lads who hung out behind the counter. He said something about me and I took it the wrong way so had to confront him about it. He said I had got it wrong, but started raising his voice at me whilst explaining himself. I told him not to talk to me in that manner but in that moment I lost my temper, grabbed him by the throat, and ended up putting him through the fridge door in a mad rush of anger. Before long I was at it again, this time with another lad who was making a fool of me in regards to my break up. He had been at it before but was now bringing in members of the public to his little comedy club, making me a laughing stock. I had spoken to John Mark, he said the same, and that the lad was starting to wind him up too, so I knew it wasn't just me. The next time I heard him have a go I gave him a quick knee, saying "Right, that's enough; you don't talk about my marriage any more, do you understand?" Even though the lad tried to laugh it off, he got the message and never bothered me or John again in regards to our personal lives. After this I would briefly explain my situation to the people who had included themselves in the banter, and say why I hadn't found it funny. Most were apologetic, saying they hadn't known the ins and outs of what was going on. I also got into a row with Joe outside the gym, but in all honesty I can't even remember what it was about now.

The void of emptiness through breaking up with Christina was now no more and had been replaced with a horrid negative anger, which seemed to cause more negative situations to come my way. The two situations I most remember took place on the way to and from the gym. The first one didn't start out my fault. I was turning into the car park as another guy in his car had started to pull in. I had signalled to go past, doing the right and courteous thing. We parked up at the same time and were getting out of our cars; me on my own, him with his wife, young daughter and son. The guy came over to me ranting on about whatever he thought I had done wrong; I wasn't sure what he was talking about so tried to blow it off, not wanting any trouble. I could feel my temper rising but knew he was with his family... it wasn't until the guy decided to start flying punches to the back of my head that I would react. We started smashing each other up for a few seconds, but my strength and force quickly left him beat. I could hear his family's cries at the back of me; not knowing what to do, and not wanting to see their faces, I just legged it back to my car and drove off as quickly as I could. I have to say I didn't have much choice with being under attack, especially with the guy initially attacking me from behind, and I'm not sure what else I could have done in this situation, but I still feel very guilty about the ordeal to this very day. The choice I made not to look at his family's faces was the best choice I ever made.

The next situation, also involving a car park, wasn't as bad, if anything when thinking back I sometimes laugh to myself about it. The car park where I used to park near the gym had a regular occurrence where people would park their cars blocking other parking bays, this in turn left you and your car stranded, waiting for the person to return so you could eventually get your car out then be able to head home. This had become quite a problem, to the point where removal trucks would have to come and shift the selfishly parked vehicles. There were some nights when I would come back to my car and the parking spot was completely blocked off so I would have to go for a walk, or just sit in the car and wait for the person to return.

One night, my car was blocked in but I thought I might just be able to get my car past without hitting the badly parked vehicle. I initially decided to wait but soon, and now frustrated, I was starting to think about what type of tool parks his or her car in this way, not caring that someone else might have commitments, or need to get home. I needed to get home for my next meal, this alone making me just pissed off enough that my concern for the other driver's car, or if I hit it or not, soon had little meaning to me. I decided I would have a go as I was now fuming, wanting to get home. I hit the gas, but within a second or so found myself wedged into the side of the guy's car, quickly realising that my judgment in distance had been a little off! I also realised that even though I was wedged quite tight I couldn't go back as there was already obvious damage to both cars. Now with a sweating brow, and a feeling of instant panic, I had to make a quick decision. "Fuck it", I thought, and off I went, the cars' metal now cracking together, with the wheels screaming as I forced my way past. I was swearing and shouting as the back end of the car finally managed to escape. I flew out of the car park like a man possessed, still shouting and bawling as I went. What a charade this had all been.

Despite this being a bit naughty I was pretty glad I'd done it, as I'd been pretty pissed off with how ignorant people could be and it was nice for once to be able to do something about it! Soon afterwards, I had to get rid of my car as the full side of it had been destroyed, this being very noticeable, but even getting rid of the car would have repercussions, as a couple of weeks down the line I was receiving letters and fines because I had not signed the vehicle off when getting rid of it. Even after paying the fine I received more letters to do with my vehicle, with an even bigger fine attached, and now threats of court procedures if I didn't pay. It turned out that the idiots from the scrap yard had run my car through a couple of red lights before scrapping it. I had no idea at the time, as all the letters had on them was bar codes rather than stating the incident, this just all added to my frustration.

The bad luck wouldn't stop there. I received yet another letter, this time from a guy who wanted to sue me for some incident that had taken place around five years earlier whilst I was working on the doors. At first I thought it was from the guy about the Christmas incident that had just passed, as he also had a pending case, but it wasn't, so now I had two accounts of assault against me... it might have been three.

There seemed to be no let-up and even with my day job the smallest things were starting to get to me. My work colleagues

Eamon and Julie would be going on about East Enders or Coronation Street, talking about them as if it was real life. This had gone on for years, but for some reason this year when listening to the two of them, I would just think them both idiots, now unable to understand their mentality. We would get into that many arguments about their conversations that eventually I would just sit out of the way, not wanting to speak with anyone, but I was still angry just knowing what shit they were talking, knowing that anything real life or factual that I might have brought to the conversation would generate no further interest.

Within months I had hardened beyond any human sentiment I had ever known.

There was one incident where Eamon and I had been arguing over something or nothing as usual, but whatever was said led me to jump to my feet, grab Eamon by his head and drag him down the aisle on which we worked. I left him on his back with everyone looking on confused, most started to laugh shortly after. Eamon got to his feet calling me names before storming off to find a manager. Luckily the manager didn't like him so just told him to sit back down and get back to work, with the situation eventually sorting itself out and everything soon going back to as it was. In fact, I think it was this incident which caused me to sit out of the way, with just my iPod for company, something I should have done in the first place.

Within months I had hardened beyond any human sentiment I had ever known. That old simple dream of happiness, good body, nice girl, blue skies, was now at a loss, I didn't think like that anymore, I didn't really think at all. I felt soulless.

With regard to training, everything was going great, my size and strength was incredible for how close I was to competition. This was the only place my high aggression levels would come in handy, but unfortunately my young apprentices didn't see it that way. Both John

Mark and young Grimes had enjoyed the earlier part of the year when we were still having the banter, I was helping them with their training, getting them the gains they had wanted. But as we got closer to the show I had them on a knife's edge when calling the shots. If they took too much time picking their weights, I would shout at them for slowing down the workout. I would ignore virtually everyone in the gym, even sometimes telling people who stopped to talk just to fuck off, no warnings. I told my training partners to have words with their friends, and tell them not to come over while we were training. I had said to both earlier in the year that when it came to contest time I might be hard work, and that I wouldn't mind if they wanted to train on their own; at the time they both wanted to carry on with me, but now they probably wished they hadn't.

Eventually I told Grimes that I was feeling guilty with how I had been with him, and that it would be best for me if he went back to training on his own for a while, we could pick up again after the contests were over. There was no argument from Grimes, he looked like he had been set free from prison! He was happy with the outcome, his 18 pound muscle gain, new-found knowledge and confidence. The young lad had come to me a boy and had left a man. Years down the line he would become a successful trainer himself and was always very thankful for the time I had spent with him.

It was a relief to be training on my own, back in my own messed-up world.

John Mark wasn't so lucky, as he was competing he would have to endure my worsening temper for a further three or four weeks. The workouts were punishing enough without me always on his case. We would be sitting on the stationary bikes most nights, I would be hard at it with sweat bursting from my head, grunting aggressively; it was only cardio but I was going at it like a psychopath. I would hear John Mark at the side of me grunting, but also murmuring on about how tough it was. He would mention it around three times before I would finally flip as he was ruining my concentration. I yelled at him, telling him that if he couldn't handle it he should fuck off home and not bother. Poor John didn't know what to think, he just put his head down and tried to plod on as best he could. On another occasion, when he had been on the phone to his Mrs about something to do with his dog, I pulled the phone off him, threw it across the room, and told him to leave his personal business at home. I later gave him a phone ban for when we were training up to the contest. I had taken a lot on with John, and now wished I could have prepped him at a different time. Being this horrid was killing me, but I had promised to get him to the show, so unless he decided to quit I would fulfil my promise, and have him ready come contest time. Despite me being a fuckin' arsehole, which I truly was, he would get his happy ending, winning both first-timers Mr England as well as the Mr UK, and had completely transformed himself in order to do this. Again, like young Grimes, John would always be thankful for what I had done for him. I on the other hand would always feel guilty for how I had been.

Once John's shows were over I let him off the hook, he had put up with enough. It was a relief to be training on my own, back in my own messed-up world. I was now struggling with work at the children's home as I could no longer interact with the troubled youths, and often ended up walking off on my own during day trips. A young lad named Jody had just started work there around this time, years down the line he told me that he had thought I was a psycho. He said that when he heard my younger sister saying what a laugh I was, about fun stuff we used to do, he thought she must be talking about another brother. He couldn't relate the character Debra had been talking about to what he had seen whilst working with me. I left the job as one day while on shift and watching TV, two mentally challenged kids started masturbating on the seats either side of me. I didn't know what to do, so just fixated on the

TV; as their noises picked up I looked around only to see the young lad's head spinning side to side while he was rubbing himself in the nether regions, with the girl rubbing herself up and down on the seat at the other side of the room, she had already left a puddle. I turned back to the TV once more, not able to address the situation. I knew after that day I wouldn't be back.

Despite all the hardship up to this contest I had managed to look well, keeping my shit together physically even if not quite mentally. I had been praying to God throughout the whole time, attempting frantically to read the Bible, but I was taking nothing from any of the stories I would read, the demons definitely taking over at this point. I had a sense of oblivion, my mind a minefield.

It was now near contest time once more. European championships, 85kg class, 2008. Lee Kemp (former junior UK champion), a guy who I had come up with in my junior years as a bodybuilder, was now a compere, and as the show I was doing was his debut as an international judge we decided to travel out together. Lee offered to put me up the night before, as the airport was only a short ride from where he lived. In the morning on waking I was anxious to get my tan on, wanting two coats applied before setting off, but unfortunately Lee wanted a lie-in and a little time to wake up, so I only got one. Lee said we would be landing in good time and would have plenty of time to deal with my tan at the hotel, so I thought fair enough, trying not to make a problem of it. The rest of the morning ran smoothly with everything going to plan, if not a touch better. Before long we were on the plane on our way into Europe.

We had been flying for an hour or so, everything on course with us now ahead of schedule, when an announcement came over the tannoy saying we would have to return home to Britain because of a problem with the plane. I was outraged! The plane seemed to be doing fine to me! I grabbed the stewardess as she went by, demanding an explanation from her as to why we were turning back, and (in an overbearing manner) telling her it was as quick to keep going forward as it was to go back. She looked at me like I was nuts, then pulled away. At this point I was fuming, ranting to myself, saying, "This is fucking great, just fucking great!" reaching a point where I was about to punch the plane. I didn't sense any danger, and it wasn't until people started putting their heads in the crash position, and oxygen masks started coming out of the hatches that I began to think that perhaps something might actually be wrong. Even then, I wasn't concerned that I might be about to die, I was thinking more about my next meal and the coat of tan I should have put on earlier. The plane was soon batting side to side, looking to be losing power with the rate it was dropping out of the sky. I knew there was a problem now, so decided to sit tight. Some of the people were in floods of tears, and

> *Lee by rights wouldn't have been out of order if he had thrown his coffee in my face*

normally this would have scared the shit out of me as I hated flying to start with, but for some reason I felt nothing. It would be a bumpy flight home but eventually we made it back, landing safely.

We were soon all off the plane, then we were told it would be another four hours until the next flight. Our once ahead-of-schedule day was now massively behind. Me and Lee went to a cafe for a drink as he started to make small talk, but I wasn't really listening and soon started on at him about my next meal and the coat of tan I needed to put on. Lee asked if I was serious. "Yes", I said, and continued ranting about him wanting to sleep in, making it his fault that I hadn't got my tan on in the first place. Lee by rights wouldn't have been out of order if he had thrown his coffee in my face, but Lee being Lee would sort the problem, somehow managing to talk whoever was in charge into getting me my bag so I could have my next meal on time.

The next bit of fun came when we decided to sneak into the disabled toilets to get me tanned up. Lee would only have to do my back and the parts I couldn't reach, so didn't have to be with me too long, so after he had done his bit he left me to it. I had been in the toilets around ten minutes tanning myself when I could hear a voice outside which at first sounded foreign, but actually on listening more closely would turn out to be a deep Scottish accent. The voice was saying what sounded like "There's a gey int toilets painting himself orange with his coke hanging out!" It took me a few seconds but then I realised the guy was talking about me! I initially froze, thinking fuck, not knowing what to do. As I turned I noticed the door had come off the latch with waiting passengers peering in at me. I quickly slammed the door. The next 10 minutes waiting for my tan to dry would be the longest I'd ever known. I kept thinking that security might be called and I'd be pulled out of the toilets and dragged through the airport with my orange arse hanging out.

We'd probably have been even more famous if the plane had actually crashed!

Luckily this didn't happen and I was able to get my clothes on, put my head down and run the fuck out of there without any more unwanted attention.

There would be no more surprises after this, and the rest of the trip went quite well. When we arrived at the venue and went to sign in, people asked if we were the British team and said they had been worried about us. They had heard on the news about our near plane crash, and it had been mentioned that the bodybuilding team travelling from England had been on board. This was the closest to famous I had felt since starting bodybuilding! We'd probably have been even more famous if the plane had actually crashed! I've got to admit I thought it was pretty cool. Unfortunately, this would be the most happy I would feel whilst on this trip as after being on stage, the contest hadn't gone how I had hoped. I ended up being placed a respectable but disappointing sixth. The final six was always a good spot to be in, but this time, with what I had been through to get there, it didn't seem like enough. After coming off stage I just sat outside slumped on the floor with feelings of mass disappointment, failure, wondering how I was going to be when I got home now my winning streak had dried up. I sat there for an hour or so before Lee came out holding my trophy, telling me the show was over and that it was time for us to head back to the hotel.

The next day Lee and I decided to go out into the nearby town; I was still very pent up despite the contest being over. I was having yet another go at Lee over something or nothing when all of a sudden my nose opened up like an espresso machine with blood gushing out onto the pavement. I think it was then that Lee started to realise that things weren't quite right with me. I think it might have been the stress of everything that caused me to bleed. I spent the day telling Lee about everything that had happened to me in the last few months, I knew I was sounding kind of crazy but Lee was a good guy and I thought with how I had behaved towards him he was owed at least some type of explanation. Lee was one of the few people who when given the chance would always do his best to help people out. He had given me guest spots and main features and photos in magazine articles, as well as promoting me as the main guy for the Federation, he would stick with me for as long as I competed. Lee was a rare loyal character, someone I would always be very thankful to.

AFTER COMING OFF STAGE I JUST SAT OUTSIDE SLUMPED ON THE FLOOR

I felt calm and at peace

CHAPTER 23

The hand of God

When we arrived back in the UK it was night time, and Lee asked if I wanted to stop over as it was getting late, but I thought I'd already been enough of a burden, so said my thanks and goodbyes before getting into my car and setting off for the long drive home. I was my usual irritated self while driving back, I needed a bit of a wake up as I had felt washed out, so I stopped at the nearest service station to pick up a takeout coffee before heading for the motorway, for what I hoped would be the quickest route home. As I was driving along I could see the road signs flashing on and off, with a queue of traffic already formed. I must admit I wasn't happy and couldn't believe there could be so much traffic on the road at that time of night. It wasn't long until the traffic had ground to a halt, and I was sitting there feeling my usual angered frustration. I soon realised I wasn't going anywhere for a while, so rolled down the window whilst making a start on the coffee.

I had been sitting for a couple of minutes when for the first time in a long time I started to feel relaxed. I found myself smelling the fresh air blended in with the freshly brewed coffee, with my thoughts suddenly feeling unhindered by the usual negativity that had been battering my head for the past eight or nine months. As I looked, I noticed my shirt was wet, even though I wasn't sweating. I realised the water had come from my eyes, even though I wasn't crying nor remotely upset, if anything I felt calm and at peace. I'm not sure if this was some kind of breakdown. But for me I would see it as God had seen me and had thought I had suffered enough, so had now decided with his mighty hand to squeeze all the anger and badness out of me, allowing me to appreciate life once more, finally being able to move on. This was the strangest thing ever to happen, but after it I was more placid, forgiving, a better person than I had ever been. Don't get me wrong, I still had my moments of madness from time to time, but for the most part I was at peace with myself and others. I had changed for the better, forever.

When I returned to the gym the following Monday, I ran into John Mark; he was talking to me, but expecting me still to be angry, as did some of the others. I tried to explain that I was OK, but it would take months before people would believe that I was. I realised that with how I had been, blending back in was going to take a bit of time. I would always be sorry about the person I had allowed myself to become during this time.

By the second part of the year things started to pick up. Lee phoned to tell me I had qualified for the World Championships in October as I had hoped. I was obviously happy about this, but after all the intense training I had done over the past years my body was now starting to pay for it. My chest felt tight, like it had a minor strain, and could possibly tear if I didn't watch what I was doing, also the tendons in my elbows, forearms and wrists were screaming at me, I was struggling with my grip and keeping hold of the weights while training. Luckily I had been spending a lot of time with a guy called Dan, who had initially come to me for advice on extreme conditioning and diet, but in the end it was me learning from him. Dan was very knowledgeable, and even though he didn't compete as a bodybuilder he had a remarkable physique, and was more committed to bodybuilding than most.

Dan formulated a training plan to help me to train around my injuries. I found the way he trained difficult initially, with the movements he demonstrated awkward. I was out of my comfort zone, as I hadn't taken any advice on training for many years. The way I had trained had been working perfectly, but now with all my injuries I would have to train as hard as I could, while trying to curb all the tendonitis which was at times agonising, reaching overload through high reps rather than heavy weights. Dan stayed with me right up to the show, and even after training with him I would stick with some of his methods, especially when training around injuries in the future. Dan was now known as Dan-the-muscle-technician-Walsh, he helped me out massively.

I met two other bodybuilders this year while starting work on a new door. The first one was already a living legend by the name of Gary Shelmerdine. Gary had been a big name in the early 90s when I had first started training; he had trained with the likes of Mr Olympia, Dorian Yates, he had made his mark as a pro competing with all the big names from the USA. He was one of the few light-

> *Don't get me wrong, I still had my moments of madness from time to time*

heavyweights who had won the overall British title, so it came as a shock one night to see him standing on the door at the side of me. He still loved bodybuilding and was still training regularly. Within weeks of working together we would both be bringing our magazine shots and telling our stories.

Gary had me strip down so he could have a look at me now I was coming close to contest. He told me that my physique looked very much like a guy named Bob Paris, and this was good for two reasons. Bob Paris was one of my all-time idols, his was one of the physiques I had most admired when starting out in bodybuilding. The second reason was that Gary had competed right at the side of Bob Paris in New York's Night of the Champions, so was actually comparing me to the real thing! This was a compliment I would never forget. Gary was like a ball of positive energy, with our love for bodybuilding magnifying when talking together. I would always feel a little star-struck by Gary, but I always loved the stories he would tell.

The second bodybuilder I met was a guy named Gareth Ward. Gareth was better known as a doorman at the time, with him heading some of Manchester's best known clubs in the past. He loved bodybuilding and had been training for six years, yet when it came to knowledge he was still very green. We would got talking and as it turned out he had wanted to compete but hadn't known how to go about it. Gareth wasn't your obvious competitor, so wasn't in great shape at the time, but he was a good guy, I could tell he looked up to me, liked my look, and trusted what I said to be gospel. I could tell he was serious, so I soon decided to take him on as my new apprentice.

Gareth's transformation was incredible, which was good, as I had filled his head with self-belief even before knowing whether he had the right tools to be able to do the job. With Gareth, I had gone on his desire, that thing in a person's eyes when he believes, that was Gareth, all heart, all fire, all desire, I would put my money on this over genetics every time. Over the next 18 months I changed his workouts in order to bring up his many weak points, as well as turning his diet on its head, slowly but surely bringing him into shape. Gareth stuck to everything I said with us becoming good friends in the process; he went on to become British Champion in the Tall Class, as well as competing at the Mr Universe, with people who had doubted him now singing his praises. He became well known throughout the North West, eventually becoming a gym manager and trainer himself. But again, like the others I had helped, he never got ahead of himself, and was always thankful for the help I had given him, which was all I wanted.

I spent a lot of time with my old friend Matt this year, he was doing well for himself running a chain of clothing outlets. We helped each other through our problems and shared a few laughs in the process. Matt's stash of old bodybuilding photos was never too far from hand, he was still very proud of his more than impressive bodybuilding heyday. I hadn't been able to drive years earlier when Matt had fallen from grace, but now whenever he was on a downer I made sure I was there for him day or night, like he was for me. I was glad I got to put right what I couldn't do anything about years earlier.

I've mentioned a lot of people during this year, the reason being that they were the ones who helped bring me back into the light, in what had been the darkest year of my life. Most of them never knew that they had helped me in any way. It felt like God had beamed these people into my life for a purpose, as they had acted as a massive positive, and at the time I most needed it. The most positive of them all, and the last person I'm going to mention on this subject being my cousin Phil Rose.

Phil had been a big influence on me since before I can remember. When we were both very young I would regularly stop over at his house, I used to talk about how I wanted to be Mr Universe when I grew up, he used to talk about going into the army, becoming a millionaire, and wanting a Porsche when he got older. There was no plan in place at the time of our conversations, these were just dreams of the moment, but magically we would end up being two of the very few who actually took their best shot at turning our dreams into reality, the way we set our mind to things very similar, however different our passions may have been.

It felt like God had beamed these people into my life for a purpose

Twenty plus years on, we were both very close to achieving our dreams. Phil had joined the army as planned, I remember going to London seeing his passing-out parade. After leaving the army he started work as an office boy with very little in the way of qualifications, but hadn't let that beat him; throughout the best part of his 20s and 30s he studied, working overly hard so (like in bodybuilding) he became very disconnected while climbing the ladder of success. Phil had been through a good few tough times himself but despite this he always remains a good father, always having strong priorities – his children came first. His hard work paid off and he became massively successful. I think at one point he owned around three Porsches, not just the one he had set out to get; he also eventually met the girl of his dreams with plans to marry her in the year 2017.

He understood what I was going through, so was always the one I most talked to, and whilst I probably sounded a little messed up, he would just listen on like nothing sounded wrong, his words reassuring, letting me know that things would work out. Phil's advice and understanding was worth its weight in gold, I knew what he had been through himself, and I also knew he had come out the other side with a smile on his face. That's what I wanted, and I could see he wanted the same for me. The second part of the year was a lot better – still tough, but the positive swing made things much easier.

It was now that time again, with the World Championship Mr Universe contest here once more. It would be the first time I would go overseas alone while competing, but I didn't mind. The contest itself went smoothly, and even though I was riddled with injuries which were now stinging even whilst posing, I was getting seen and receiving some good call-outs when on stage. I knew my efforts wouldn't be in vain, unlike earlier in the year. I placed fifth, making this the biggest success of my international career so far. For the first time in a long time I felt like my life and career was finally back on track, and was even optimistic about the year ahead. I had finally come to terms with being on my own, now able to move on with my life.

> **I had lost friends, my marriage, and nearly my mind**

Christmas turned out pretty good; Phil had me out most weekends, eating at all the nice restaurants, sitting in the VIP sections of all the posh clubs or bars, and as I didn't drink I was designated driver – which wasn't so bad as I got to drive his Porsche! My injuries were slowly but surely on the mend, and I was now able to ease up a little on my training. My solicitor, Stuart, who was also a friend, sorted out all my legal problems which I had put to one side while competing, so after a couple of court appearances I was back in the clear.

I spent Christmas Day alone, as family parties weren't really my thing at that point, but I did go out on New Year's Eve, meeting up with my younger sister Debra. It was a good night, but as the night drew on nearly every pub or club we went to had doormen I knew telling me that Christina had been in the venue earlier, or that I had just missed her. I felt a little upset up on hearing her name, and I have to admit that I thought there may be a brief moment were we would meet, then kiss come the midnight hour, I kind of hoped for it in a way; but it wasn't to be, so instead I was shaking doormen's hands and toasting a drink with my sister as the new year came in.

This was the last time I went out in my home town. I knew my feelings for Christina were still there, so I would have to stay away, I even made it known that if any of my friends saw her about, I didn't want to know. My head was more or less right now, so I couldn't allow anything to change that, not now life had just started to feel good again.

By 2009 I felt a lot more at ease, and just with that the world seemed like a better place. I was enjoying gym life once more, with the banter back at an all-time high. I wasn't competing until mid-season, as I had already secured a spot at the Mr Universe come October, so I could now relax a little in terms of cardio and diet. I had wanted to start pursuing other aims – bodybuilding was still my main love, but it had taken its toll. I had been dieting and training without any kind of let up for the best part of two years and had now been in competitive bodybuilding nearly twenty. I had lost friends, my marriage, and nearly my mind in the process.

My training was going well, but my training partner Dan had started training elsewhere, having only stayed until I had finished my show out of respect for me. Now I was relatively injury free I was on the lookout for someone to take Dan's place. Training partners at this late stage were very important, they would have to tick every box; that's why I would spend a lot of time training alone. Training partners would have to be prompt, virtually never miss a workout, they would have to know when to talk, when to train; they would have to spot perfectly, to the point where you didn't know they were helping but you would still be moving the weight. I would have to respect them in the way they trained, but still I would want to call the shots. They would have to be positive about what they were doing, as well as be able to keep up in both pace and weight. As I found out, a good training partner would be the one who could challenge you, but would also want the best for you. My only sales pitch was guaranteed results. This wasn't easy to come by, but by around early March of this particular year the right guy for the job would come along.

Even though I had never trained with Rob Lyons in the gym, we had been at the same fight classes together for the past four or five years. We had been pretty closely matched in terms of training and the amount of punishment we could take, including both body and head conditioning, with us never leaving anything behind when sparring against one another, both going hell for leather, neither of us backing down. I wasn't sure whether this would be the same while training with the weights, but fortunately it was. In no time at all our training had gone through the roof but even though very intense and heavy, it was good fun too. We used to wind up young Grimes, and his new training partner Phil Vyas, saying they were pussies, forcing them to lift heavier – then we would have to beat their weights, just to annoy them. The banter was rife, but everyone seemed to like it. I had set myself up as the gym ego, with everyone getting on board; there was a new crowd of young lads who had been around the gym, their personalities second to none, they all loved the daftness of it all.

Not everyone found it funny though, especially Alex. Alex was at a stage where he had started to take himself a touch too seriously. He would play grunge metal whilst in the gym, which no one liked, but worse than that, he used to scream during every set – and I mean scream. We would all be kind of laughing but not saying anything... anyway, there was a guy by the name of Tom Bates, he was a wrestler, but liked to do weights. He started yelling "It's a boy" whilst Alex was screaming during his heaviest set, and also making vomiting noises, comparing it to Alex's music. Everyone was pissing themselves, apart from Alex, who would usually have a rant before walking off in a huff. The situation did sort itself, with the two of them actually becoming training partners as well as good friends somewhere down the line, it was a lot of fun. Even though I can't really get it down on paper, these were really good times. After the year I'd had, I was more appreciative of laughter than I had ever been.

AFTER THE YEAR I'D HAD, I WAS MORE APPRECIATIVE OF LAUGHTER THAN I HAD EVER BEEN.

CHAPTER 24

Every dream met but one

Out of the gym, things were also going well. I had been doing acting classes in the hope of maybe getting seen in a few things. Starring in a film was something I'd always wanted to do, and by sheer luck, I got my chance. Dan, who I had been training with throughout the past year, was also into acting and had sorted some acting classes, whilst guiding me through the process of eventually getting an agent. He was part of a prestigious acting school, so already had his own portfolio and agent sorted. His agent had recently been in touch, wanting Dan to try out for a new British movie that was being shot in the Manchester area, based around a two-bit loan-sharking theme. Dan had gone for the part as one of the loan sharks, but unfortunately had not looked right for it – he ended up getting a part as the gym instructor.

He had been asked if he knew any lads who would fit the description for the loan sharks, and had quickly said yes, with me in mind. When Dan told me about the role I jumped at it. I was off-season so was full and powerful-looking; even though I would rather have been in shape for the role it was the full-faced menacing look that the director wanted. After Dan sent the director, Simon, my mug-shot it wasn't long before he got back saying I had the part. Dan also asked me if I knew someone tall in stature, and sinister-looking, to play my partner in crime, and I chose my up-coming apprentice, Gareth, to take on the role.

We were on set for two days, with day one being short and

sweet. Me and Gareth had to intimidate some guy in a back street, throwing out a few swear-words whilst grabbing him by the throat. It was only simple stuff but we enjoyed it all the same, I couldn't wait for our next scene. The next time we got the call it was at a large house somewhere in Manchester, with a professional camera crew all set up as we drove in, so on arriving it felt like the real deal. We were taken inside and while getting our makeup done I noticed a famous face. She was an actress named Michelle who had stared in a string of soaps as well as few decent Brit flicks back in the 80s. She wasn't particularly chatty, and wasn't like any of the characters she had played, she was actually quite posh and came across as being well-educated. The next famous face we noticed was an actor named Paul who had starred in the cult classic movie Dead Man's Shoes; he was easy to work with and came across as a good guy. Our first scene involved our characters breaking into the house, we were filmed walking around the house, looking like we were trying to find someone. In the next scene we stood next to Paul as he made a threatening speech to Michelle's character.

I got my moment of glory, as I had to deliver a stunt punch on Michelle. Although earlier Michelle had seemed reluctant to speak, as soon as we started to practice she was at no loss for words, telling me about her newly veneered teeth, and how she wanted the stunt punch to land around a foot away from her face. I knew how close I could get it, but played it down until it was time to shoot the scene. The time had come, Michelle was looking at me very nervously as we stepped up to do our scene. Simon the director shouted "Roll", I moved into position and without a second's notice quickly flung a speedy hard right, straight in the direction of Michelle's face. Michelle fell over backwards, and the crew looking on thought she had actually been hit, I could hear their gasps right after throwing the punch. It only took a couple of seconds for everyone to realise that she hadn't been hit, then the gasps turned to laughter. Afterwards, some of the crew came over, saying that they thought I had really hit her, telling me how exciting yet funny it had all been.

It might have been my one and only scene but I had made it look real, it would have definitely been the story of the day. The day had been great, this being something I had wanted to do for a long time, with the stunt punch being a massive added bonus. The cast and crew all said their goodbyes, they had made us feel really welcome as had Simon the director. Unfortunately my new mate Michelle wasn't for saying goodbye, she stood glaring with a look of madness towards me as I left the set.

Another dream I had wanted to fulfil also came to pass this year, something I had wanted to do from being very young. I had recently joined Facebook, it was great for hooking up with a lot of my old friends, which in itself was a good thing, but I had also hooked up with some of my old crew from way back when I used to dance. Breakdance had been my first real passion when I was a kid, my dream being to break in the company of the best dancers in the world, which back in my day would have been the Rock Steady Crew. Paul Morris, one of the guys from way back, was trying to organise a Street Level reunion (Street Level being the name of our old breakdance crew). Luckily, while getting the old crew back together Paul found out about a massive dance event taking place in nearby Manchester. Some of the world's most famous dancers were going to be there. It would also include a tribute to the old school, featuring three of the original Rock Steady Crew, the most notable being Ken Swift, who had danced in the movies Beat Street and Flash Dance.

There were originally six of us in our crew but only four would eventually show. On hearing about the reunion I started practicing, in the hope that somehow my dream of dancing with the Rock Steady Crew as well as some of the newer dancers might somehow come to pass, even though I wasn't quite sure how. Some of my friends were sceptical, saying I was living in a dream world, and with the size that I was, they didn't think I would be able to dance at all. Everything I had ever done had been based on dreams, but with dreams you first have to put things into place for if you ever get the chance of bringing them to life. For a month or so up until the show I would do two or three 20 minute sessions a week, in order to get a decent dance run together. I wasn't even a third as good as I had been as a kid, but I still managed to get an acceptable old school run, so was pretty happy with myself considering I was nearly 15 stone at the time.

I knew I might not get the chance but I always believed anything to be possible, and even if I just ended up watching the show, I would still be glad of the brief glimpse of youth I had been able to revive just in how I had practiced up to the event. This was the beauty of having a healthy body and a healthy mind, you could always go back, still being physically and mentally capable of doing things most people couldn't. Even if you had learnt what you had learnt 25 years or so earlier, it would never prove to be a problem. Mental focus was the key, and I had learned to use it better than most for the things I wanted to achieve.

The day would come with four of the original crew turning up, Ste Rammy, Paul Morris (formerly Burdakie), Louise Burke and of course, me. The show was a blast, seeing all the best dancers from all over the world brought a massive rush of adrenaline, and when watching the old school tribute, a lot of great memories came flooding back, taking me back to the fondest of times. After the show only me and Paul from the original crew decided to stick around, and it was a good job we did.

Paul got talking to a guy he used to dance with who had also been part of the night's show, the guy then invited us back to the after-show party. The dream was getting realer by the minute. When we got to the party, the scene couldn't have been more perfect. All the dancers had formed a circle, all busting their moves. Ken Swift and a couple of the other old school legends were all taking part, all I had to do now was have the guts to jump in there. I slowly made my way to the front. I had asked Paul to get a shot of me on the dance floor with Ken Swift in the background, I just needed the bottle now to get into the circle. I stood for a while and even though the guys' moves were unreal I realised that yet another of my prayers had been answered, it was now up to me. I was nervous, but knew how angry I would be if I didn't at least have a go. With this, even though scared half to death, I thought "Fuck it", and as soon as Ken Swift had been on I decided to make my move.

The run went well, I could hear Paul shouting for me, with all the other dancers spurring me on and clapping as I was throwing myself around the dance floor. As I got up I shook Ken Swift's hand before making my exit. Paul said everyone had been cheering, I think they were impressed that a 15 stone 35-year-old was still gutsy enough to get up and be able to bust a few moves, or at least that's what I hoped they thought. Paul flicked through his camera then showed me the shot of me in the air with Ken Swift in the background; it was the perfect end to a perfect evening, with another one of life's dreams met.

For me, it had been a good year, but for a lot of people, especially those who don't like moving house, it might have been a nightmare. I had been living in Matt's house while doing it up, but the house was now on the rental market and was attracting interest – so it was time for me to move on. I couldn't go back to my mum's as they had just started redecorating, but money was tight, I was paying solicitors' fees whilst my divorce was still pending, as well as paying for my car, so there was a choice to be made: rent a place to live and have to scrimp on eating, supplementing my diet properly; or eat well and have nowhere proper to live. I decided to take the second choice and to live off God's good grace for now.

Breakdancing with Ken Swift

An acting
role for the
big screen

It was time to see what the
judges would think

CHAPTER 25

Living off God's good grace

It was early spring, with the weather just starting to come warm, so initially I decided to live out of my car as I had no intention of signing up for a flat or a house, and wouldn't have been able to afford the deposit even if I had wanted to. I had my clothes hung up in my car with my mum doing my washing when needed. As I had no microwave, fridge, or any other household appliances, I would have to get into work early then literally spend the best part of an hour every two to three days cooking a shed-load of sweet potato and chicken breast, bagging up what I needed for the day, keeping the rest in the work's fridge for when I needed it. There would be a couple of complaints for the first couple of weeks or so as the canteen had stunk, people were asking what was all the shit on top of the microwave and why it smelt so bad. Now and then I had to explain my situation, and how it was just until I could get some money together, or find somewhere cheap to live. There were still a few complaints about the smell, but in general most people didn't push the issue, leaving me to get on with it. I kept my eggs in the car along with my porridge oats, shaker and water, so I could mix together a few shakes in the morning and again at night after training.

I found sleeping in the car comfortable enough, actually preferring to sleep upright as opposed to a flat bed a lot of the time, but for the times I felt like bedding down, I had kept the keys from the garage of the house I had been staying at, for when it came time to pick up my stuff, so sometimes I would sneak in late at night and use an old mattress that was already in there to get a decent night's sleep. None of this bothered me for some reason, driving somewhere quiet and scenic at the end of the night was actually quite pleasant. I was like a trainee tramp and felt I was doing quite well at it!

From early 2009 up until around August I moved in and out of places around seven, eight times; from when I first split up with Christina I had moved 15 times in total. It went from an empty house, to stopping at friends' places while they were away on holiday, a couple of short-term house shares, right through to living out of my car, and derelict, run down, houses whilst in between digs. Sometime in August, when my car had been paid, and my divorce finalised, I was able to get a place of my own. I'd enjoyed moving from place to place, meeting different people as I went, telling people about my situation. It wasn't quite the norm, and I could sense that they felt a bit sad for me at times, but I would always make light of the situation, saying I was like the dog from the TV series The Littlest Hobo – I would even sing the title track to make them laugh, to show I was actually quite happy living this way for the time I'd had to.

> *from when I first split up with Christina I had moved 15 times in total*

Despite all the house moves my training hadn't faltered, I don't think I missed a single meal throughout the whole time I was on the move. In August I moved in to my own little pad, just in time for when contest prep was starting to get serious, also in good time before the winter months started creeping in. The apartment was only small but I loved it, it was cosy, with the building itself feeling very welcoming, looking like a manor house from the outside. It was situated right at the side of a picturesque little town that had its own steam train. The little town ran Sunday markets and various other events. The surroundings were hills, parks and rivers; this was the perfect spot for me, I felt instantly settled upon moving in.

The contest prep was well on the way with both Dan and young Alex telling me just to enjoy coming into shape rather than killing myself. They said I was already in good shape so should just go with it. This seemed like a good idea – it was something I hadn't tried before, as well as being something that wouldn't compromise my sanity.

The contest prep went well, I came in that little bit heavier with good condition to boot, and even though I still preferred my obscure final touches as I thought they added that little bit of something to my overall physique, for now I would keep with the plan. It was time to see what the judges would think, on what would be my fifth Mr Universe appearance and sixth International overall.

Unlike the past couple of years, we had a strong team. There were a string of famous faces including Martin Yates, Neale Cranwell, Mick Hehir and Brandon Marjoram. At the hotel checking in I was stood behind Neale. I knew he was a professional who took the shows seriously, so hoped I would get partnered with him. Unfortunately the rooms were in set order so Neale ended up on his own with me paired up with the classic bodybuilder competitor. Initially when getting to our rooms the guy seemed OK, we even arranged to keep coming back to the room every three to four hours to help each other with our tans, as well as getting each other's

They said I was already in good shape so should just go with it

opinion on how we were both looking. I didn't actually leave the room, and never did the day before a contest unless I had to, but my roommate seemed keen to get off. Four hours went by with no sign of him. I needed to get a coat of tan on in order for it to dry ready for another coat later in the day. It was all carefully timed so running behind would be a problem.

Luckily Neale turned up at my door, he was actually looking for my roommate who had also promised to help him but instead had disappeared, doing his own thing. Me and Neale sorted each other out, then made arrangements to help each other throughout the event. When we stripped down we had quite similarly shaped upper bodies, but Neale's was on a larger scale. He remarked on my condition, saying how dry I was. My upper body looked a touch harder than Neale's, but when you saw his legs you could see why he was cleaning up at all the major contests – they were of perfect shape, shredded, dry, with his whole physique in general symmetrically flawless, he truly was a class act.

Later that night I was rudely awakened by my roommate clanking about, banging doors. It was around ten at night and he was only just starting to unpack, he had not been back to the room all day. He was farting, burping, not making any effort to reduce his noise level. I soon started to get pissed off and asked politely whether he could unpack in the morning as I was trying to get some rest before the contest the following day. He apologised, saying he wouldn't be long, but even after going to bed he was still constantly farting, burping, the room now smelling like shit and bad breath. I knew sleep was out the question but I kept quiet, trying not to make it a problem, doing my best to keep the peace. I realised that the guy as well as being a let-down was also disrespectful. If the previous year's version of me had been there I would have thrown him out of the window by now, but this time I would just have to deal with losing a night's sleep.

> *If the previous year's version of me had been there I would have thrown him out of the window*

The day of the contest arrived and played out without any problems. I had come in good shape, very dry with muscle well refined in detail. I weighed in at just under 85kg, which was spot on, however I didn't look as full as in previous years for some reason, especially round the chest and sides of my legs, even though the fronts of my thighs and inner thighs had vastly improved. In the line-up I held my own size-wise, and was without a doubt in better shape than the rest of the class, so I thought that on this day I might be getting my first break into the final three at a Mr Universe contest, but after a season of call outs as usual I was none the wiser about my placing. I placed in the final six on this evening but only the top three were announced; once again I hadn't been selected. I hadn't questioned the judging of this show before, but now I had my doubts about a few things, it definitely seemed like there was bias amongst the judging panel. Both Neale and Brandon had won their

> *I hadn't questioned the judging of this show before, but now I had my doubts*

classes, but they had been stand-out winners. Brandon had dropped a weight-class but was shredded, with him looking a lot larger in the lighter class. Neale, on the other hand, had looked perfect, as a lot of the other heavyweights had full, bloated waistlines, with a watery appearance to their physiques.

It wasn't long before the answer came to me, but it didn't come in time for me to make use of it. The answer was that in order to win at this level I would have to be the clear winner. I had been slightly better in both condition and shape for this contest, but I could still be easily judged down, and without any English judges could quite easily have slipped a few places. I had no answer at the time as I had tried every technique known to man when it came to final prep, going balls-to-the-walls every year, improving as I went. I thought I couldn't have done any more but knew I would have to if I wanted to come up with a winning plan. For now my mind was at a standstill.

The show was over, so after a sleepless night the night before, I was looking to get a decent sleep. When getting back to the hotel I had a little to eat before calling it a night. Around one that morning, when I was in a deep sleep, my disrespectful roommate returned. Banging, clattering, farting... and this time he decided he was going to take a shower. Don't get me wrong, I was a better person than I was the year earlier, but still I wouldn't be putting up with this kind of shit from anyone. I sprang to my feet and without any explanation, grabbed him by the back of his shirt, hurling him

it was now time to travel to the place I had always dreamt of

from the bathroom, through the room where we slept, and out of the door. I quickly said something about losing a night's sleep the night before and how it wouldn't be happening again, then I slammed the door, with him yelling "I'll go back to Angela's then, you bad-tempered bastard!" from the other side of it. At this point I felt like opening the door and running at him, but was quick to calm down, laughing about it shortly afterwards. This was my first bad experience when it came to sharing a room, but at least I'd had the last laugh, got rid of the idiot and was able to get back to sleep before the journey home the next day.

On getting back I had only two weeks at work followed by two weeks' leave. I thought with it already being such an incredible year, and me still being in shape, it was now time to travel to the place I had always dreamt of from being young, California USA. I sorted the whole thing out the week before, only booking flights; my friend Simon would sort out the first couple of days' accommodation, as well as the car hire, the rest of the stay would be travel with no tie-ins, which was just how I wanted it.

DON'T GET ME WRONG, I WAS A BETTER PERSON THAN I WAS THE YEAR EARLIER, BUT STILL I WOULDN'T BE PUTTING UP WITH THIS KIND OF SHIT FROM ANYONE.

California was everything
I had hoped for

CHAPTER 26

California USA Where all my childhood dreams began

California was everything I had hoped for, and as soon as I had dropped my clothes off at the hotel I was off to check out Venice Beach, the place where all my dreams and motivations had stemmed from. There was the bodybuilding side of things, but also my first two great passions, breakdancing and skateboarding, had also stemmed from the beach.

On hitting Venice Beach it was just like it had seemed in the movies. The first place of interest I spotted was the original Muscle Beach; this was the site of the original Mr Universe contest where such names as John Grimek, Reg Park and even Sean Connery had competed back in the day. The beach looked unchanged from the 1930s with the gymnastic hoops and parallel bars still in place. I thought I'd make my first workout an old school one using the early apparatus from the original school of bodybuilding. As I left Muscle Beach I could see an area of space that I recognised only too well, it was where the dance-off from the movie Breakdance had taken place. I recognised it instantly as I had watched the movie that many times while growing up; I remembered the scene clearly, also remembering a young Jean-Claude Van Damme clapping away in the background. Moving on, I saw the outdoor gym from Pumping Iron, which had featured both Arnold and Franco Colombo. This all seemed so surreal to me, it was hard to get my head around, knowing that by the next morning I would be training in the same spot where both bodybuilding legends had trained while shooting the documentary, I couldn't wait.

As I walked further up the beach I could see a place known as Dog-town, one of the largest and definitely most noted skate parks in America. As a kid I had always wanted to come here and skate with the pros. I had actually brought my skate board with me in the hope of having a go, fulfilling yet another long-awaited dream, but on getting closer now, gazing into the huge concrete bowl, I could see that the pace of the skaters was rapid, with none of them falling off, which I would definitely be doing after nearly a 20 year break. So for now at least I would have to leave this dream on the back burner. This was only day one, I was buzzing; I couldn't believe what I had already seen, and that despite all the history, as well as the well-known people to do with all the obscure sports I had loved while growing up, this place was still so easily accessible, most of it being free or just pocket change to use. Back at the hotel that night, I couldn't wait to get started on the next day.

The next day, after loading up on a couple of meals I was off down to Muscle Beach. I used my skateboard to get around, hoping that if I was on it enough I might have the confidence to brave Dog-town at some point. As I got to the outdoor gym I realised it had just opened. The guy who worked there asked if wanted to leave my skateboard whilst I trained, which I did, and as we got talking, I found out the guy had come from England. After only a short conversation he said I could train there for free while I was over, which seemed mad as I thought it would be expensive with how well-known the gym was.

After training for around 15 to 20 minutes I was pumped, now in full bloom. I would say the only real time bodybuilding is easy is the couple of months following a contest, when you've filled out massively yet are still in good shape. It was amazing to be in California, being seen this way, a massive added bonus, my arms over 19 inches at this time. In-between sets tourists would be taking snapshots with some of them actually wanting to come where I was and have their picture taken with me. I soon realised that I was the muscle on Muscle Beach that day, and was now a tourist attraction! I thought this was brill, I loved every minute. Yet another dream had come to pass.

> *I soon realised that I was the muscle on Muscle Beach that day*

An elderly guy, who had been looking on, approached me then asked if he could take some shots of me after I had trained, to which I said yes. After my workout, whilst in-between shots, he was telling me that only the week before, it had been the 75th anniversary of Muscle Beach, and Arnold himself had been there giving a talk on how much the place had meant to him, still showing support to his bodybuilding roots. Also the current Mr Olympia, Jay Cutler, had been there doing an outdoor shoot, the guy I was talking to was one of the photographers on board. He was telling me stories of how he had taken photos of Arnold back in the day, then he asked me if I wouldn't mind him using the pictures he was taking as part of the feature he was doing on the 75th anniversary – which more than anything I was flattered by.

I asked him if I could have a copy of the photos but because of copyright, and the fact he was working for a magazine, he had to say no, but he didn't mind if someone using my camera wanted to duplicate the shot in the same spot; so a young lad who had been looking on proved only too happy to offer his services. The general public was looking on whilst doing the photo shoot, I felt like a superstar making the most of the great experience, enjoying this day to the max. The guy asked later if I wanted to be part of some kind of carnival, but I had to decline as I would be travelling up the coast on the day it was taking place, but thanked him for his time as well as the compliment of featuring me with some of the greatest names in bodybuilding, whether I would be seen in the magazine or not.

A couple of years later I would see the Jay Cutler shots from Muscle Beach, they were shot in the same format as mine had been. Even some shots of a young Arnold had been shot in the same way, with similar lighting and angles, which made me wonder whether the same guy who had been responsible for some of the classic Arnold shots had been the one taking shots of me on that day – with him being the right sort of age it got me thinking. After finishing the photo shoot I got talking to some of the locals who had been around at that time, they told me stories of Arnold, how he had lived on the beach when he had no money, with some of the locals opting to feed him, sometimes taking him in. They pointed to a hotel, and a particular room that both Arnold and Franco had rented when they first started making money. I seemed to remember an old picture of them both leaning on the balcony. I knew when I got back from my round trip I would try to rent that same room.

> *I could see why no one was staring at him, he was proper scary-looking*

The guys told me where both the original Gold's Gym and the newer, larger Gold's were both situated, so it was now time to check them both out. It was only a couple of minutes' walk before I could see the original Gold's Gym. This legendary gym was abandoned, with bars on the doors and the original sign partially worn. It seemed odd, if it was me I would have kept it open as a museum, I was gutted I never got to go inside. A couple of blocks down, I saw the new Gold's. I say new, but I think it had been around since the late 70s or early 80s, so it would still have seen a lot of the big names I had looked up to when first starting out in bodybuilding. I wouldn't go in on that day, but checked out the opening times so I could return the day later. This was the last gym on my tour of gyms that I had wanted to train at, so again, I couldn't wait, already excited about the next day.

By the time the sun was rising the next morning I had already eaten and was making my way down to the beach. It was Thanksgiving and lines were forming as on this day everyone could get a free dinner. There were loads of street shows going on, the place massively alive. I'd never met such friendly people. After enjoying the festivities as well as my free turkey dinner, it was time to get to the gym. On entering I could see it was an active gym, everyone very serious about their training. I had people I didn't even know saying I looked good, being very complimentary towards me as I wandered through the gym. I started working out, just finishing my first set, when two well-known faces caught my eye. The first face was Lou Ferrigno, aka The Incredible Hulk. He was in a corner actually working as a personal trainer, just blending in with everyone. This seemed strange as around 10 or 15 years earlier on his comeback tour I had waited 20 minutes just to shake hands with him, in Gold's there was only me looking on.

The next famous face I saw was old-timer Robby Robinson, he had starred in the original Pumping Iron, and was something of a legend after winning the heavyweight over-40s and over-50s Mr Olympia title, possibly having the longest professional career in bodybuilding history. I said "Hi" to him as he walked past, he just looked, smiled then said "Hey Man" as he walked on by; he was the coolest man alive.

I would see a few more famous faces, including Dennis Hopper who had been just sitting and staring at me as I trained, I'd not been sure who he was until I had left the gym, I kicked myself about it later. Another guy was Jonnie Jackson, a modern day pro known for his awesome strength, I could see why as he was throwing 80kg dumbbells around like a warm-up weight. I could see why no one was staring at him, he was proper scary-looking as well as being absolutely massive at the same time. Gold's Gym had been quite an experience.

After leaving the gym I had dinner, then decided to walk over to the skate park as it was dusk with the park now half empty, so I thought there might be a chance for me to have a go. As I got to the park I could see there were still a few skaters about so decided to go to the back, where it was quiet. I got to skate the street part of the park but the bowl still looked daunting, but then I thought because I was travelling up country the next day this might be my last opportunity to give it a go. Unfortunately I still wasn't ready, eventually bowing out of skating the huge bowl. I felt a little down and defeated as I left.

The next day came with the road trip about to begin. I picked up my Ford Dodge from the car hire place and blasted off up the highway. I would cover over 1,000 miles on my trip, stopping off at Santa Ana, Santa Monica, San Andreas and Santa Cruz before reaching my ultimate destination, San Francisco. I travelled all day, rock ballads and open road, only stopping for sleep when tired. I drove over San Francisco's Golden Gate Bridge while it was still dark, just as the sun was starting to rise with the bridge still beautifully lit. I slept for a couple of hours, then took on the day. I'd only been driving a couple of minutes when I had reached the foot of one of San Francisco's massive hills. I had wanted to bomb up these hills ever since watching the movie The Rock, starring Nicolas Cage. It was still quite early, and no one was around... soon I was bouncing down the streets as if I was in the movie. I got a bit carried away at one point, with the car taking off from the road, skidding on landing, and missing another car by an inch or so, it was all pretty mad.

I parked next to the Golden Gate Bridge, knowing I would always be able to find my way back to it, the bridge was so big that it was never out of sight. Walking along the bay I could see what looked like a distant floating tomb set in the cold waters, surrounded by rising mist, this was a place I had always been fascinated by, it was Alcatraz. Before long I was on the ferry paying the place a visit. The stories about this prison were amazing. The likes of Al Capone had served time there, I listened to his story whilst sitting in what was once his cell. I spent the rest of the day in San Francisco seeing all the sights, taking rides on the trams, finding out even more about the place as I went. When at last it was dark I decided it was time to drive back down to Venice Beach. I didn't want to waste any time so I drove back overnight, stopping off for a short sleep along the way.

soon I was bouncing down the streets as if I was in the movie

After dropping the car off early I was straight back down to Venice Beach. My first port of call was the hotel where Arnold and Franco had stayed. I asked the guy at the counter about which room the two legends had stayed in, and luckily enough it was available! Now I was staying in the same room as the greats once did, and I could see why they had liked the room so much, as the views from the large open window looked like a painting, the skies perfect. As I chilled out that evening I could see the skate park from the window. There was something about not skating that bowl that wouldn't stop bugging me, I already sensed the regret I would have if I wasn't at least to give it a go.

The next morning, on waking, while it was still quite dark, I went straight across to the skate park. When I got there, there was a guy vacuuming leaves out of the bowl. When we got talking I found out he was an old time pro named Jesse. He had done the British skating tour the same time I had, nearly 20 years earlier. Even though he didn't remember me, he remembered some of the events we had both done. Jesse was a big name back then, he had been winning most of the major contests, and like me it was more about the passion for the sport rather than what he could gain from it; now, being warden at the park was still his idea of heaven.

Speaking with Jesse had made me feel more at ease about the task ahead, it was time to attempt the bowl. I hit the bowl, trying to pick up speed in the hope of grinding out the top of the larger bowl. After a short while a guy approached me, he was talking about which hip to hit, then how to gain speed, he then showed me what he meant by giving me a demo on his own board. He was with me around 40 minutes but even though I was getting closer I was now getting smashed up quite bad. I had fallen off several times and had friction burns all down my legs, arse and back, with the blood now starting to show through my shirt. The guys from the side were egging me on – I was like a man possessed, trying to grind the top of the bowl. I was in agony, but I had come so far that I knew I wasn't going away until it was done. Finally, after a lot of pain, I was able to grind out the top whilst managing to keep on the board. All the guys now laughing and clapping,

"You're one crazy guy; you'll fit in round here!"

then one of the guys said "You're one crazy guy; you'll fit in round here!" They thought I was nuts, it had all been a lot of fun.

The guy who had helped me had now set off down the pier to get some breakfast. One of the guys asked me how I knew Christian, I said I didn't know him, he had just seen me struggling and had decided to help. Then I found out that my coach had been a guy named Christian Hosoi, a pro skater from back in the day. I had admired him, even had posters of Christian from when I was young. I couldn't believe it, it was the perfect end to the perfect holiday.

Although seemingly non-relevant to bodybuilding, all the events that had happened in this year had taught me that anything was possible. There was the USA trip, where you would just have to get off your arse, save up a little, then get there. Some of the other things, like my little movie role, would come about by chance, just by showing interest. Both the breakdancing and skating were the sort of thing where you had to work at it a little, but were still possible if you were fit, focused and prepared to put yourself through what was needed to do them. Everything was about fulfilling long-awaited dreams, with the dreams still being true enough to you in order to want to live them out.

I had filled a bucket list full of dreams this year, but my most wanted dream had still eluded me; the Mr Universe. On getting back I started racking my brains, trying to think of the one missing ingredient, the finishing touch that could give me the edge over next year's competition, but nothing at this point would come to mind.

Over Christmas I ran into Christina when on a night out, and right away a lot of forgotten feelings came back to haunt me. She was with her friends, but I found myself just standing looking over, then in moments our eyes would meet. Her eyes were still the beautiful blue they had always been, but were now emotionally drained, donning a slight redness, with a look of both sadness and disappointment clouding her once innocent, pure sparkle, the upset very clear and upsetting to see. There was a wall of hurt between us as we both stood staring at each another. I felt angry at myself for the upset I had caused. This was the start of an on-off, sometimes turbulent affair that would last through from Christmas 2009 to the summer of the following year.

Despite the relationship with Christina, bodybuilding was always going to be my main focus going into 2010, with both myself and Alex discussing our careers over our regular coffee outings. I was talking about immense condition – even though I had always been sharp in the past there was always that 5% of competitors that were sharper. I wanted that look but without compromising too much size, but wouldn't be able to take the chance as long as I was competing in the under 85kg weight class. I was facing a dilemma.

California - trip of a lifetime

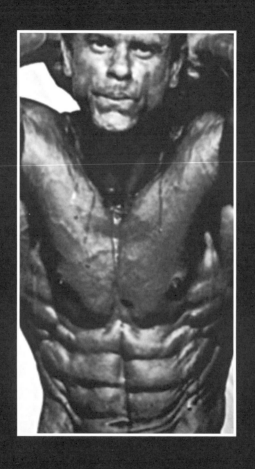

CHAPTER 27

Two world championships back to back More determined than ever

By early spring 2010 I had received invitations to do several international shows, I'd never actually realised just how many Federations there were! I hadn't heard anything from Lee, who I had the most loyalty to, so I decided to go for a Mr Universe I had placed quite well at years earlier. The show had been stopped three years earlier as some young lad had dehydrated, suffering a heart attack whilst on the trip home from the show. The organising guy said it had now become a professional event, so only top national or international competitors would be getting invites, this would lessen the risk of anything happening like that again, or I presume that was the reason. He said the class was still a height class, but due to the weight differences now being harder to judge there was going to be a split in the height classes, with the class I was doing being the lower weight of 82kg and under. I'd been competing at around 83-85kg, so this wouldn't be too much of a drop, if anything I could come in that bit lighter and tighter as I had hoped. I said yes, signing up to do the show, so now I had a plan with a contest to aim for.

Matters would soon be complicated – as soon as I signed up for one Mr Universe, Lee was on the phone asking if I was competing with him. He said I had the choice of which class I wanted to do, but that they hadn't got a middleweight so asked if I would be interested in dropping down to a lower weight. He thought I might want to step up to the challenge, he also said he couldn't see anyone beating me if I was to make the weight. I quickly thought it through. The Mr Universe Lee was promoting was three weeks before the one I had already signed up to do. I thought that if I had to get down to 82kg for the second show then in order to carb up fully I would have to get down to at least 78kg – if I could get down to that weight I would be ultra-shredded, to say the least. Even if I was to flatten out at the first show I would have 7kg to fill out

> *I knew if I could do it, the possibilities would be limitless*

before coming in for the second, with this I could be back up to my fullest, as well as tightest to date. I took a couple of minutes to deliberate, but eventually agreed to do the show and at the lower weight. Game on.

Having to drop 9kg from my already ripped physique was bad enough. 9kg was around 21 pounds, which is tough to lose even when it's just fat, but when it's all muscle it's like breaking down steel with a wire brush, but I knew if I could do it, the possibilities would be limitless. Living on my own I spent a lot of time studying, reading a lot of scientific books to do with nutrition, as well as the supplementary books that most bodybuilders read. I had all my books stacked up on shelves, I even had a couple at the side of the toilet for when I had to spend time there. Even though I owned a TV and a DVD player, I would never connect the TV, as I didn't want to waste time watching useless programmes, keeping my head in the books instead. I only ever turned the TV on to watch movies or box sets I had fancied. I spent more time formulating the perfect diet plan this year than ever before, and even midway through I was constantly changing things to suit. I studied a lot about supplements that helped keep focus, as well as keeping a balanced mind, speeding metabolism without having to add excessive calories. Without getting too scientific, I had worked out every way and portion to deal with the kind of diet and training I was about to undergo, so even before I had started my diet and training plan, my knowledge of my sport was at an all-time high.

By around June, I was already training hard, adding aerobic work to the end of my workouts, even though it was still very early in the season. I'd changed my workouts, so on what would normally be my off-days, I would work in a day where I would only do hamstrings and calves, in order to make them a stronger, more detailed body part, as my hamstrings from the rear needed more width and separation, and I thought this the best way to sort the problem. My back had always been my strong point, so now with all the weight I had to lose, I thought it best to lose it from there, as it would still look good no matter what, and if my back was trimmer it would make my hams seem thicker. I was now 100% symmetrical from the front and side, but wanted also to look the same from the rear – I wasn't far off but it would now have to be right. I was my own worst critic, so was going to make sure I was my fullest, tightest, and perfectly symmetrical from every angle.

my knowledge of my sport was at an all-time high

I trained my abs every day. Taking the weight off the waist would only make me look better, and if I trained them every day they would never quite recover. This meant that they would always be slightly over-trained, causing the waist to shrink yet still look shredded, this would also make my thighs appear bigger. I would do the same routine with my back. Every time whilst out doing my cardio, power walking through the park, I would throw myself up on the climbing frames to do as many chins as I could, all this as well as already training back twice a week in the weight room. This way my back would always be slightly over-trained. I was hoping to take the weight from my back with it being my strongest body part in order to get to the weight class needed but without taking it away from my overall balance. It was a good plan but was still going to be tough.

In my personal life Christina and I had been on and off now for around six months. Our once very close relationship was now more about bodily needs and familiarity, with a string of turbulent fallouts and spats of hate coming into play. I had been unattached mentally even before dieting, and now that I was well into my contest prep, this had become more apparent. Meanwhile, Christina had also become much more independent herself. I think with us both, the anger that had generated was coming from how good things once were. Things weren't like that any more, we both knew it, but hadn't wanted to admit it to ourselves in the hope that the situation would put itself right somehow.

after the last of many fall-outs we would both agree to go our separate ways

In the end we were falling out over such stupid stuff – like, one of her friends had seen me at a car boot with Julie a year or so earlier – and even dafter stuff about a spiritualist telling her I was going to get her pregnant, not want the kid, then steal her money! It was getting ridiculous. The truth was that our relationship was well and truly over, so after the last of many fall-outs we would both agree to go our separate ways.

I was well into my contest prep, but nearly two weeks after we had finally split, I got a text from Christina, saying we needed to talk. At first I thought "What?" and then "It can't be?" But it was. Christina was pregnant. I was a little shocked, nervous, sceptical, not completely sure if she was telling the truth. I said I would need a day or so to let it sink in.

I rang Christina the next day, saying I would be there to father the child regardless of whether we were together or not. My original plan had been that after finishing bodybuilding I was going to take off to the USA to pursue a film career if possible, but being moral in my ways I would always put human life before anything else, especially as this new life was my creation, my responsibility. If I was to have a child I would make sure I was there to raise them, regardless of previous plans. In fact, having my own child was the only thing that would have stopped me from moving away.

> *the more time that went by, the more disconnected with my personal life I became*

Christina and I agreed to stay separated but also agreed to stay friends, so once, twice a week I would pop round to see her, to show my support. I kept my bodybuilding life and my personal life separate, but the more time that went by, the more disconnected with my personal life I became.

It was only July, with both world championships taking place in November, but already I felt the pressure. I was weighing in around 82kg, more ripped than ever, with most people at the gym thinking my show must be only weeks away! By August I was stripping down already having the wow factor, with the plan of reducing my back and waist size working accordingly. I was high-dosing on L-arginine as it gives fuller muscle pumps as well as reducing fatigue, I also used taurine as it keeps the mind focused. Rob, my training partner, knew my way of training well, so there were never any problems there. My waistline had reduced to around 27 inches, it looked freaky when posing, making my thighs and shoulders look enormous by comparison. I had already dieted and trained up to this point as hard as I would have up to any contest in years previous.

With still having a lot of weight to lose, already in shape, I had started to get worried so tried seeking help from other competitive bodybuilders who had dropped weight classes whilst competing, including my old mentor Rob and a guy I had competed with in recent years named Brandon. Both the two, even though looking like death whilst competing, had only dropped 4 or 5kgs, so while offering their best advice they couldn't be of any real help. Now I knew I was on my own, with the road ahead starting to get dark. If In past years I had watched such films as Rocky and Youngblood for motivation, now I switched to movies like Black Swan and Gattaca.

Gattica's lead character was played by Ethan Hawke and it was about a guy who hadn't had the right genes to make it to a more privileged life, but through working extra hard, as well as not messing up in any way, he managed to fool the system, being able to make it to where he wanted to be. The caption for this movie was "There is no gene for the human spirit," which I loved, and even though the film wasn't anything to do with training, it meant more to me than any other film I had ever seen before. Black Swan, starring Natalie Portman and Wynona Ryder was very much the same; although it was about ballet, it showed the depths and anguish a person would be willing to go through to reach perfection, even if it meant dying for. Like both the characters from the movies, I wasn't going to accept anything less than perfection, no matter what the outcome.

> *I wasn't going to accept anything less than perfection, no matter what the outcome*

I was around 10 weeks out but was still around the 80kg mark. I was ripped to bits, dry to the bone. I'd be losing around a pound every two to three weeks. As well as a three-hour outdoor walking duty at work I would also be doing hours of cardio. My cardio involved power-walking and running up steep hills first thing in the morning, with another full hour on the weights, followed by 90 minutes on the ergo-cycle at high intensity, later on in the day. At this point I was down to 50 grams of complex carbs daily, filling the rest of my meals with empty low-glycaemic carbs, mainly raw broccoli, my main source of protein coming from egg whites.

I no longer had the capacity to function with the outside world. When attempting to talk I would constantly be slurring words. Sometimes during conversations I would be talking very slow, mumbling, missing out bits of conversation while trying to explain something, so even though the answer was going over OK in my mind, I would be forgetting to actually speak, and not even knowing I was doing it. People were worried about what I was attempting to do, with me now starting to sense it. I was eight weeks out from my first contest, and Christina was 12 weeks pregnant.

PEOPLE WERE WORRIED ABOUT WHAT I WAS ATTEMPTING TO DO, WITH ME NOW STARTING TO SENSE IT.

CHAPTER 28

The heart beat

It was the day of our baby's first scan. Up until now I hadn't really taken it on, and even on the day I was only half expecting to see a live baby, with part of me expecting to see nothing at all. I knew if the baby hadn't made it, or if it had been a phantom pregnancy, it would break Christina's heart; but for me, although I might have been a little saddened, I don't think with how I was that it would have made too much of a difference to how I felt.

Now in the hospital. Christina was on the bed, and the woman carrying out the scan was rubbing the scanner over Christina's stomach. The picture on the screen was much the same as the last time, you could see the shape of the baby but no movement. It was like déjà vu, the woman again, like last time, saying to give it a second. Christina's face had gone white, her once smiling face turning serious, I too was feeling anxious. It was the longest minute of our lives, but then, all of a sudden there was life, our baby quickly flipping over, almost as if to see what was going on. The lady now showing us in full view, telling us our baby was very lively and healthy, she said the baby must have been sleeping when we had first looked.

I had been a distant uncaring cyborg when I walked into the room, but now I felt elated, my head and heart pumping with excitement. Christina was also in full bloom, both of us laughing like little children knowing we were going to be parents. I hadn't smiled or felt like this for a good while, a real natural high, knowing the baby was real, healthy, very much alive, and that by the same time next year I would be a dad.

We went for lunch that day, the sun was shining, I took it as a sign of good things to come. Even though I only had steak and salad my spirits were lifted, with us both talking about names and things we would have to buy for when the baby came along. We had kept Christina's pregnancy a secret, saying we wouldn't tell anyone until after the first scan. I had only told Alex, my cousin Phil and my sister Debra, as they were the people I was most close with. Christina had wanted to blast it from the rooftops, but I had to ask if we could keep it secret until after the contests were over, as I knew people were already starting to talk. I didn't want them on my case, seeing me so messed up, knowing I had a child on the way. I also asked Christina not to get on my case herself, as I knew how distant I was going to be, but I also promised that when the shows were over I would be 100% on board with both her and the baby. Christina agreed, and to be fair she never complained once, even when I came round and sometimes never spoke at all. The pregnancy thing really worked for Christina, I barely ever saw her upset. I think she actually enjoyed being pregnant, which was good for me as I don't think I could have dealt with any type of negativity coming from anywhere at that point, there was still a lot to get through before show time.

> *I didn't want them on my case, seeing me so messed up, knowing I had a child on the way.*

I DON'T THINK I COULD HAVE DEALT WITH ANY TYPE OF NEGATIVITY COMING FROM ANYWHERE AT THAT POINT. THERE WAS STILL A LOT TO GET THROUGH BEFORE SHOW TIME.

now everything seemed
like a challenge

CHAPTER 29

Time to dig deep

I had booked three weeks off work prior to the contest, as this was the time when I usually started to struggle. However, I had already been struggling for the past month or so, and there were still another five weeks of work until my leave. Already work felt seemingly impossible with my functioning skills already at zero. I knew most of the people on my post round, but now a couple of the residents started asking if I was all right, saying I looked stressed. My mate Phil, who lived on the round, would come to the door as he always did when wanting a chat, but when I saw him I would just say, "Can't talk Phil, can't talk", walking on by without even moving my head. Luckily he understood, as he trained himself so knew what I was like come contest time.

On my round I was counting the streets, the corners, the paving stones, now everything seemed like a challenge. Once, when delivering the mail, I had been munching on turkey and some broccoli, holding the food in a small bag underneath the mail as I walked. I had delivered the handful of mail, not even noticing the turkey and broccoli had gone until I went to take a bite at the end of the street – I soon realised I had put the food through someone's letter box. Next thing I was walking back up the street trying to remember which house it was, so I could knock on and ask for it back. Sometimes, half way through the round, I would just go and sit in my car for 20 minutes or so, my head spinning, barely knowing where I was, needing a little time just to get my head straight.

When I visited Christina I would barely speak, if at all. I had to sit away from her, any type of contact or closeness wasn't for me. I

LIVING THE NIGHTMARE **BECOMING THE DREAM**

actually couldn't bear the thought of anyone touching me, let alone giving me a hug. Christina would always be excited, telling me how she was, showing me her baby bump, as well as all the things she had bought for when the baby came. Even though I sensed her excitement I never felt it myself.

We had kept the baby news a secret from most – or so I thought. But one morning at work Julie saw me slumped over my work station, head in hands. She asked how I was feeling, but in an abrupt kind of manner. She obviously had something to say. "Don't you think you should be looking after your lady at this time, not just thinking about yourself, can you not see the state you're in, John? It's not just about you any more. Sort yourself out!" And that was that.

> **"Can you not see the state you're in, John? It's not just about you any more. Sort yourself out!"**

I wanted to yell at her but knew I would probably black out or fall off my stool if I did, so just ended up sitting there glaring as she swaggered off in her usual, I've-got-a-bee-in-my-bonnet attitude. Julie was one of my favourite people on the planet but I must confess there were a couple of seconds where I had envisioned strangling her, as I was fuming about her approach, but I think I was more angry because I knew she was right, and that was the reason I had kept the news so secret in the first place. From now on I knew that other people around me would also know, so with this, I started hiding myself away even more, taking my break in the disabled toilets, ignoring everyone or pretending I hadn't heard them, to the point where everyone knew not to approach me at all any more.

I felt the guilt of knowing I had a child on the way, along with the feeling that something could go wrong, both mentally or physically, but I also sensed the regret I would feel if I was to give up, having come this far, I knew it would eat away at me for the rest of my life. I thought, when the time came, how would I be able to talk to my child about not giving up on the important things in life, if I had done it myself?

I think the notion of dying doing something I loved always appealed to me in a certain exciting yet morbid way. I would have liked that. But knowing I had a child on the way, something new to live for, that could no longer be the case. Still, regardless of the outcome, I couldn't and wouldn't quit. In fact, knowing that life was going to change after this year, I wanted to push myself even harder. I knew that once I hit the four week out mark I would be OK, as I had planned to have a blow-out meal at that point, in the hope that it would rev my metabolism in order to get the last few pounds off. At the same time it would allow me a little more body and mind energy to get through the week, which would be the last week before taking leave from work. I would consider this my safe zone; it was just about being able to get to there now.

> *I think the notion of dying doing something I loved always appealed to me*

Including work, I was doing around six hours a day aerobics, as well as an hour a day on the weights. I was only taking 20 to 40 grams of carbs daily – any normal person needs at least 100 grams, just in order to function, that's without any added exercise. So you could imagine the state I was in after doing this for several months. I was spotted in Bury sitting amongst a group of old ladies all chatting with each other, as I'd been so tired I had just plonked myself in the middle of them, completely unaware of my surroundings. Even the likes of Steve Grimes, who I had trained with years earlier, would mention that he had never seen me this way, and said he preferred it when I was the horrible bastard shouting the odds – he was worried about my welfare. I was more scull than skin at this point, my blue eyes peering and distant looking. I was rarely, if at all, aggressive, however I would still prefer my own company.

I had broken away from most people, even my sister Debra looked upset while in my company. I wasn't particularly worried – it was only when talking to people, and seeing how they looked at me, that it would get me slightly on edge. I actually felt more sorry for them than I did for myself. The only people I met up with in the latter stage of my contest preparation were Alex Clarke and Phil Rose. They were the only two people I could talk to who didn't seem worried, who knew me well enough not to analyse or question what I was doing, knowing I would do it anyway.

There wouldn't be much let up, but on Sundays after starving myself all morning as well as going for a three hour cardio venture in the hills, followed by my weekly weigh-in, I would ritually jump on the tram into Manchester. I would enjoy a jacket potato with cottage cheese, also allowing myself milk in my coffee. Chilling, sat outside a coffee shop with a hot milky cappuccino, would be my idea of heaven; it brought a nice gentle release of energy, enabling me to enjoy my day with full thought. From around early September I had started buying Christmas presents, as well as little toys for when the baby came.

> *it was only when talking to people, and seeing how they looked at me, that it would get me slightly on edge*

Although I didn't want to be in the company of the people I most cared for, I was thinking of them fondly when picking their presents. This perhaps seems like a strange pastime for a hard core bodybuilder, I can't actually remember how it came to pass, but it would be some of the most enjoyable me-time I would ever have. I had always been a thoughtful person, but with every passion, addiction, obsession, a person can sometimes be consumed, appearing very different, sometimes frightening, but the person you are deep down will always be in there somewhere.

I managed to get to the four week out mark, so could enjoy my well-awaited treat, in the hope of a massive metabolism boost as well as a couple of days of added energy. I decided it would be curry takeout on this occasion. After waiting anxiously for nearly an hour, the food had arrived. On eating the food, I soon noticed it wasn't for going down, it almost felt like it had lodged rather than digested. I ate most of it, but it wasn't sitting well, so come midnight I was vomiting it back up. My plan of being fuller and happier for the next couple of days wouldn't come to pass, if anything it had left me feeling more drained going into the final week at work.

> *I vaguely remember thinking, "An ambulance, what for?" – even though at this point I couldn't move*

I made it till Wednesday, but it felt like an eternity. I was out on my post round as usual when without any warning my legs went from beneath me. One of the locals from the estate was asking if I was OK, and I replied that I was, while slowly getting back to my feet. I walked a couple more steps before finding myself on the ground once more, the local now stopping whilst looking on. Half way back to my feet, once more, I had slumped into the fence, but this time everything appeared blurred, my heart racing but with me now unable to get up. I saw the local on her phone, she told me an ambulance was on the way and I vaguely remember thinking, "An ambulance, what for?" – even though at this point I couldn't move or speak. The small ambulance came and a paramedic brought me round with some type of drink. She advised me to eat something, then go home and get some rest. I told the doctor that it was diet-related so she made an appointment for me to see someone later that day.

Luckily for me, the lady specialist who saw me knew what she was talking about. She said eating so little for such a long time had caused my digestive system to shrink, which would explain my now 25-inch waistline. She said that even though my system would expand a little when eating or drinking, it would be some time before it would return to full size, and that I would have to eat steadily otherwise the vomiting would carry on, adding to my illness. Even when eating normally, the illness and the vomiting might still occur randomly from time to time for possibly up to six to eight months. She advised me to come off the diet, then offered to give me a diet plan which, although still low in content throughout the day, would leave me having my biggest meal later on at night to keep my digestive system open for longer as I slept.

The next day I decided I wasn't going to take the specialist's advice.

I called in sick for the rest of the week which took me on to my three weeks' leave before the contest. The next day I decided I wasn't going to take the specialist's advice. I just thought that now I was off work I could carry on as normal, and could deal with my health issue when the contests were over. But on the very next day I collapsed in my doorway as I came back from my cardio, cracking the top of my head on the door whilst looking for my keys. I came round about four hours later, not quite sure what had happened. This time I felt shaken and a little afraid, so I decided at least for now and over the coming weekend I would stick to the diet plan the specialist had set out for me, just to be on the safe side. It felt good allowing myself the extra calories, eating my soft, warm, Weetabix with honey while wrapped up in my quilt watching my favourite Corey Feldman movie, The Goonies. It was literally just what the doctor ordered.

IT FELT GOOD ALLOWING MYSELF THE EXTRA CALORIES, EATING MY SOFT, WARM, WEETABIX WITH HONEY WHILE WRAPPED UP IN MY QUILT WATCHING MY FAVOURITE COREY FELDMAN MOVIE, THE GOONIES. IT WAS LITERALLY JUST WHAT THE DOCTOR ORDERED.

With the reaction I got
it was as if I had just
performed a mind-
blowing magic trick

CHAPTER 30

Looking to find the winning edge

That Saturday, when I was working the door I was more sociable, able to speak, obviously through the extra calories. I got talking to a guy I used to work with, telling him about my coming show. He told his girlfriend, and a couple of people he was with, what I looked like and before long was on my case for me to open my top so they could all see. I took a minute but then just zipped down the top and started to flex. Happily they were all blown away with what they saw, even some of the club punters were looking on with a small crowd now starting to emerge. With the reaction I got it was as if I had just performed a mind-blowing magic trick, but the only magic on this night was me and how I looked. I'd never had a reaction like this in all my career so I knew that at this point I was looking extra special, just like I had hoped.

Monday came around with me no closer to solving my little digestive problem, but luckily and only by chance an idea came to mind. Now I had finished work I would start my walks much earlier. We were into early October, so with the weather being much colder, I had as usual switched to bottling up hot water while out on my walks. As I glugged the first pint, I noticed that my veins had started to stand out, indicating that my body's blood circulation was moving much faster, also causing my inner organs to open and my body's temperature to increase. This being the case my metabolic rate would have also elevated, so right away I started wondering whether, if I were to drink a ton of the stuff, spread throughout the day, and even at night, would this be enough to cure my problem, as well allowing me to start shedding the pounds again, at least until the contests were over? Luckily it was, so from that day right up to the contest, I was swilling around 15 to 18 litres of hot water daily. I had to spend a lot of time pissing but because I was out so early I could go when and where I wanted. I would only have to do this for three more weeks, problem solved.

> *No longer would I feel like the weirdo, as from now I was in my own self-obsessed little world, I couldn't be happier.*

At this point I had lost contact with everyone, so didn't have to deal with worried faces or people whispering about my private life. No longer would I feel like the weirdo, as from now I was in my own self-obsessed little world, I couldn't be happier. The morning cardio around the old town then out through the country park was bliss, listening to old rock ballads, thinking about the coming Christmas, the warmth of the festive season. Mostly I would be thinking of the child I was about to have, already having predicted it to be a boy, that's what I always wanted. One frosty morning I was listening to a track on my iPod but for some reason the words from the song sent my mind into the most positive of realms. The band's name was Daughtry, and these were the lyrics:

> "It's not over, I'm going to put it right this time around
> It's not over, there's a part of me still standing in the ground
> This love is killing me, you're still the only one."

Suddenly I was thinking about my relationship but in a positive sense, many thoughts flooding back. I didn't know when or how, but I knew then that I could make things right again between me and Christina. The iPod was be on shuffle, and the next song went:

> "I'm going home to the place where I belong,
> Where your love has always been enough for me"

... right away I kind of smiled then looked towards the sky, my thoughts saying "God, I've got the message." As a small sparkle of sunshine glimmered through the trees, I felt inspired, this was a good moment for me. I was now more tired than ever, but my frame of mind was at peace. I now had a sense of looking forward to my coming future with great optimism.

I DIDN'T KNOW WHEN OR HOW, BUT I KNEW THEN THAT I COULD MAKE THINGS RIGHT AGAIN BETWEEN ME AND CHRISTINA.

CHAPTER 31

Loving God and looking forward to fatherhood

My early frosty walks were the best part of the day, the part I most looked forward to. Going to the gym was now difficult, keeping the heavy weights moving whilst virtually zero-carbing. I was eating broccoli, egg whites followed by a teaspoon of oats, my power obviously suffering, but luckily my mind was still strong enough to get me through what I had to do. I would go to the gym wearing six or seven layers of clothing, just to keep some kind of body heat, which wasn't easy now the weather had turned frosty, with me down to an estimated two per cent body fat. My sweat ran cold no matter how hard I pushed it, the sweat appearing like water, with no texture nor odour to it. I mostly ignored the morning crowd, as they would only want to mither me, trying to find out how I looked like I did. Trying to keep body heat was already hard enough without people slowing me down. The only guy I even attempted to speak to was a gym veteran named Lee Owen, as his smiley face and positive attitude always managed to raise my mood. He would only want to know how I was.

Back at the apartment I would have my meal followed by an hour's sleep. On waking I would strip down in front of the mirror throwing down a litre of hot water, which would instantly bring out all the veins. I could see the vein which connected in my neck then would try to follow the same vein to my ankles. I wasn't looking at my abs, I was more interested in the connective tissue surrounding them. I was looking at the depth of split in the muscle, my aim being to look like an anatomy chart with a thin layer of skin thrown over the top. I would spend an hour posing, putting together my routine, before finding the need to clean the house, and would always take my time whilst washing up as I liked the feel of the warm water on my hands. For the rest of the evening I would read, eat the scraps of food I was allowed, before watching an episode or two of a box set I had just bought called Dexter. This series was about a moral serial killer who lived a normal life, the character is very much disconnected whilst also quite disturbed, so you can see why I warmed to the character at this time. I would sometimes attempt to watch comedies but would just end up sitting there wondering what the fuck I was watching, not knowing how I had ever found this funny, my perception of things very different to when in everyday mode.

> *My closest friend was God. I would speak to him regularly, and for long periods of time.*

My closest friend was God. I would speak to him regularly, and for long periods of time. God wouldn't hear my muttering broken-up conversation, only my thoughts and dreams, he would hear and I would feel the calm welling on speaking with him. More than ever I knew it was he who had given me the strength to get through what I had to. He was the positive light to my every day.

The days played out like this right up until contest time. On the morning, the day before the show I went down to the gym for the final weigh-in. I had starved myself from teatime the day earlier, it was now around 11am, the next day. I was hoping to have made the weight, but on stepping on the scales I weighed in at 78kg - still 8lbs above the target weight. I felt gutted as I knew there was no time left, as it was only a matter of hours before having to set off. I drove down to Mansfield that evening, staying with friends Mike and Joanne the night before the flight. From arriving at their house until arriving at our destination a day and a half later, I ate only one turkey breast cut up into small portions. I also had to cut my water massively in the hope of drying out enough to make the weight.

I must have appeared quite crazed and anxious. I kept talking to Mike about making the weight, mentioning it a ridiculous amount of times. In large crowds or when stuck in queues I kept grabbing Mike's sleeve, with him just looking at me a little oddly but not saying anything – I was that afraid of getting lost, I knew that if for any reason we were to get separated I wouldn't be able to find my way to anywhere. I also thought that I might collapse, another reason for not wanting to let them out of my sight. The two would have to look after me like a child throughout the whole trip, and I'm really not sure what they thought of me at the time, I'm just glad they thought enough of me to put up with me at my weirdest.

As we arrived at the venue, I was instantly looking to where the competitors were weighing in, anxious to get on the scales. When my turn came, I was that afraid of not making the weight that I stripped down bollock-naked, not caring what people might think, just hoping I would make the weight first time. I stepped up to the scale, covering my frazzled little pecker as the scale's digits slowly turned. Bingo, I had made the weight! This was like winning the show itself. The crowd around was laughing, but they weren't shocked, as I'm sure a lot of them had been through similar themselves at some point. I then legged it off, clutching my undies, so I could quickly get back, get carbed-up, then hopefully get some rest. Within seconds of getting back, I was into the oatmeal, trying to fill out for the next day's contest. What a mad rush it had all been.

all eyes were on me

CHAPTER 32

Politics at the judging table and little team morale

The Mr Universe, 2010, round one. Contest day was finally here, everyone getting ready backstage. On taking my shirt off, I soon realised that all eyes were on me. The carbing up was working wonders, filling me out dramatically with me now weighing an astonishing 82kg, looking clearly bigger and tighter than anyone else in the class. One of our guys, who wasn't competing but had come to help, was on the phone and I heard him mentioning that the middleweight looked shit hot, meaning me. I was really pleased. It had been close but I had cracked the look I wanted, so truly felt I would be competing for the title.

The contest rolled on with us all on stage. I had seen myself as the winner, but the callouts were all over the place. Although I knew who would be the finalists there was still no clue as to who would win the contest, or even be in the final three. As I came off stage I was none the wiser, so would just have to wait for the night show to find out. I was tipped to win, with everyone I spoke to saying first, or at the very worst second. Mike was so sure that he said he would wait behind with me at the overall.

Mike was a great lad, but a lot of the other competitors on the British team weren't such great team players, and I caught a few of them talking behind my back — I was sitting just a couple of rows behind them but obviously they hadn't noticed. They were referring to someone wearing a different tracksuit than the rest of them, which I had done as I didn't want to wear a hoodie, wanting a tracksuit that slipped easily on and off. I soon realised it was me they were talking about. One was going on about me not talking to anyone, saying I thought I was better than them, another was saying that if I didn't want to be part of a team then I shouldn't have come.

The last comment, and my favourite, came from the guy I had shared a room with the year previously. He was saying what an arrogant prick I was, telling them the story of when I had launched him out the room the year earlier. I found it quite funny when listening, but the fact was that most of these new wave self-promoting arseholes, so called bodybuilders, had better genetics than me, so were having a much easier ride than I ever had. They didn't know or care just how much being at this kind of level meant to me, or just how long a time it had taken for me to get

a guy who was part of team USA just said "You got fucked there, bro"

there, and what I'd had to sacrifice in the past to do so. After listening to them for around 10 minutes or so I decided to go over. I bluntly asked if any of them had anything they wanted to say to me, not one of them saying a word, just sat there all sheepish. I stared at them for a moment, before walking off to sit elsewhere.

The start of the final night show was here, I heard roars of upset as various final judgments were made with a lot of the spectators showing their disapproval. So far none of our lads had been placed where they thought they should have been. I was backstage talking to Mike and the junior, Mike was saying he thought I would get the victory regardless, but the junior, now bitter at his own placing, was saying that he thought I deserved it too – but looking at the judging so far, there was a good chance I might not even make the final three. I tried not to listen, but as we walked out to the front I could see the judges arguing quite abruptly with each other, and the American judge yelling, "You can't keep voting for your own country, it's not right." It looked as if it was more about politics than who was actually best; still, I hoped with how I looked that I would be seen as the clear winner.

My turn came around, and as the fifth place contender was announced, my hopes were just starting to rise, but seconds later, I heard my name, fourth. Not only had I not won, I hadn't even made the final three. I dipped my head in disbelief, I didn't even bother staying on stage to listen to the final announcements. As I came off stage, even the foreigners who never really said much were telling me I was robbed, they were shaking their heads, patting me on the back as I passed by.

I knew a lot of people had been annoyed by the result, various comments were coming my way with the only one I properly understood coming from a guy who was part of team USA, who just said "You got fucked there, bro," as I was leaving the venue. I was upset, there was no denying it, it was good to know that virtually everyone had seen the result as I had, but still that wasn't going to get anyone to change their mind or give me the title I so rightfully deserved. France, Germany, Spain and Italy would dominate the top scorers of the day; they had also been the dominating judges too.

That night, when getting back to the room I realised that I had gone through most of the bottled water. There was only around one and half litres or so left, which would have seemed like a lot, if I hadn't been passing bucket loads whilst on the way up to the show. My body was at the stage where it was used to that amount, and was still trying to pass that similar amount back out. By around midnight, I was trying to ration the water, but I was passing twice as much as I was putting in, and starting to get worried. I was suffering severe tiredness, but wanted to stay awake to make sure I was putting water into my body and at regular intervals. I was tired, hungry, and not able to think too straight. The story from the show I would be doing next, about the kid who had suffered a heart attack through dehydration, was playing on my mind.

I tried drinking the tap water, but it wasn't for going down, and the kettle in the room wouldn't work, so I couldn't boil the water either. I started to panic, and took a walk to see if I could find other competitors' rooms, but all lights were out, and apart from Mike and Joanne who barely had any water themselves I wasn't sure where anyone else was, so I went back to my room, not quite knowing what else to do. I kept drifting in and out of sleep, forcing myself up when able, walking round the room aimlessly in a desperate attempt to stay conscious. I was praying to God, as I always did when panicked, but in the end, I was sitting on the bed with my eyes and my mind in virtual shutdown.

As I sat staring at the bedside cabinet, the answer to my problem appeared. Right in front of me was my mobile phone, which had a clock as well as a built-in alarm, which I knew about but had never used. I set the alarm to go off every 25 minutes throughout the night, then went to bed with the bottle of water at my side, so I was sure to take a swill every time I woke, continuing this ritual throughout the night. Admittedly I wasn't of sound mind, maybe I was being paranoid, but still I was glad that I had gone with my instincts. I gave thanks to God on seeing the sun rise, for giving me the answer I had needed to get me through the night safely.

I thought that after a healthy breakfast, with lots of fruit juice and jams, I would feel OK, but for some reason this wasn't the case. Throughout the whole journey, and even on the last leg of the trip, I would feel no better, with my battered, strange ways and slow washed-out movements still in play.

On the journey home Mike and Joanne wanted to stop off at the services for something to eat, deciding they wanted to sit for some KFC. I wasn't sure about it, fearing that the salt might leave me dehydrated. Even though I had downed around five pints of water, I was still convinced that dehydration was my problem. But I really liked the thought of KFC, so now pretty much starving, I decided to indulge. The soft salted chicken tasted like what could only be described as a slice of heaven. On eating a second leg, I felt my body heat begin to rise, with the blood flowing into my muscles now starting to fill them out, even my battered brain would instantly feel fully functional.

Suddenly I now felt excited like a crazy kid, and from virtually not speaking I was ranting on to Mike and Joanne, telling them how the chicken had made me feel, and how I thought it would dehydrate me, but it hadn't. Both Mike and Joanne were telling me that it probably wasn't dehydration – through all the water I had taken in, my body's natural electrolytes might have just dropped too low, so they now took me over to the chemist to get a couple of weeks' supply of replenishing body salts. My only thoughts at the time were that my run-down state would hopefully be sorted, I didn't know that these salt sachets were about to play a big part when going up to my final show.

I WAS PRAYING TO GOD, AS I ALWAYS DID WHEN PANICKED, SITTING ON THE BED WITH MY MIND IN VIRTUAL SHUTDOWN.

I knew I had hit on
something, something
that once again could
give me that edge

CHAPTER 33

Could the KFC bucket hold all the answers?

The week later I had to go back to work, as my holiday allowance had stopped short, not enabling me to have the full run I would have wanted, but it wasn't a problem as my diet was now much higher in content. I decided I would take the salt sachets into work, throwing one down before getting started. Around 20 to 30 minutes after taking one, I felt just like I had after eating the KFC. My body started to warm up, and again I could feel myself starting to pump up. Curious to see what effect it was having, I locked myself into the disabled toilets and stripped off in front of the full length mirror that was in there. I was blown away, I could see that the salts had not only forced the blood into the muscle but had filled the muscle out beyond any type of pump I'd ever had at the gym, also leaving me looking dry and tight. I knew I had hit on something, something that once again could give me that edge, all I had to do now was bottle the process in order to get to the next contest.

On the Friday that week I wanted a second opinion as to how I looked after taking the salts, so I knew it wasn't just me thinking I was better than what I was. I drafted my old pals Roger Bentley and Karl Bleakly, as both had trained and had been around bodybuilding since way back when. One by one we sneaked into the disabled toilets for the viewing, hoping we weren't seen. As I stripped down

I was watching their faces, hoping for a positive reaction – then I saw them smiling and nodding, the look of approval shining from their faces, I knew I'd cracked it. Karl came to speak to me later, saying he thought that this might be my time, he also said that Roger wanted to get back in the gym himself, having seen me. I was now feeling excited about the whole process, I knew I would just have to nurture it, and with another two weeks off work running up to the show, I would have plenty of time to do so.

The two weeks that led to the show went by quickly. I had Sarge (my pal from the gym) keeping an eye on me. I had used higher carbs for the first couple of weeks, as knew this would spike my insulin, hopefully enough to salvage some of the muscle I'd had to strip whilst training for the first contest. I would now have to drop back on the final couple of days in order to tighten everything up. On the latter end of the final week I again wanted a second opinion as to how I looked whilst using my peaking method, which was now perfected. I was viewed by two old-timers Sarge and a guy named Nick Cambell. They both said the same thing, that I'd nailed it. They commented on how flawless my shape, symmetry and condition looked, again comparing me to the likes of the legendary Frank Zane and Bob Paris. They saw me as I saw myself, and I was happy with this outcome. It was now just a matter of getting it right on the day.

It was a long flight, but through having had little sleep the night before I was passed out for the better part of the trip. Again, like the last show, even though I was able to put on a whopping 7kg, I was still nearly 2kg over the 82kg weight limit, so was sipping water and eating small amounts, right up to when we arrived at the venue. At the weigh in, I just managed to slip in a fraction under the weight, which was just what I wanted, I would now have the day to replenish.

There was only a small team, three competitors, and Mike, a guy I had competed with years earlier but who was now organiser and judge for the event. On arriving at the hotel Mike had asked whether I wanted to share with one of the other competitors or have a room to myself. I opted for the single room, as buddying-up hadn't proven too good for me in the past. If I had opted to share, I don't think on this occasion there would have been a problem, as the lads on the team were very professional, they had come to compete, and although quiet, were also very courteous and complimentary in their ways, my kind of people. In the room alone on this occasion, although it was quiet, come the night time I was unable to sleep, feeling very anxious about the day ahead, just hoping that everything I'd put together would come right.

THEY COMMENTED ON HOW FLAWLESS MY SHAPE, SYMMETRY AND CONDITION LOOKED

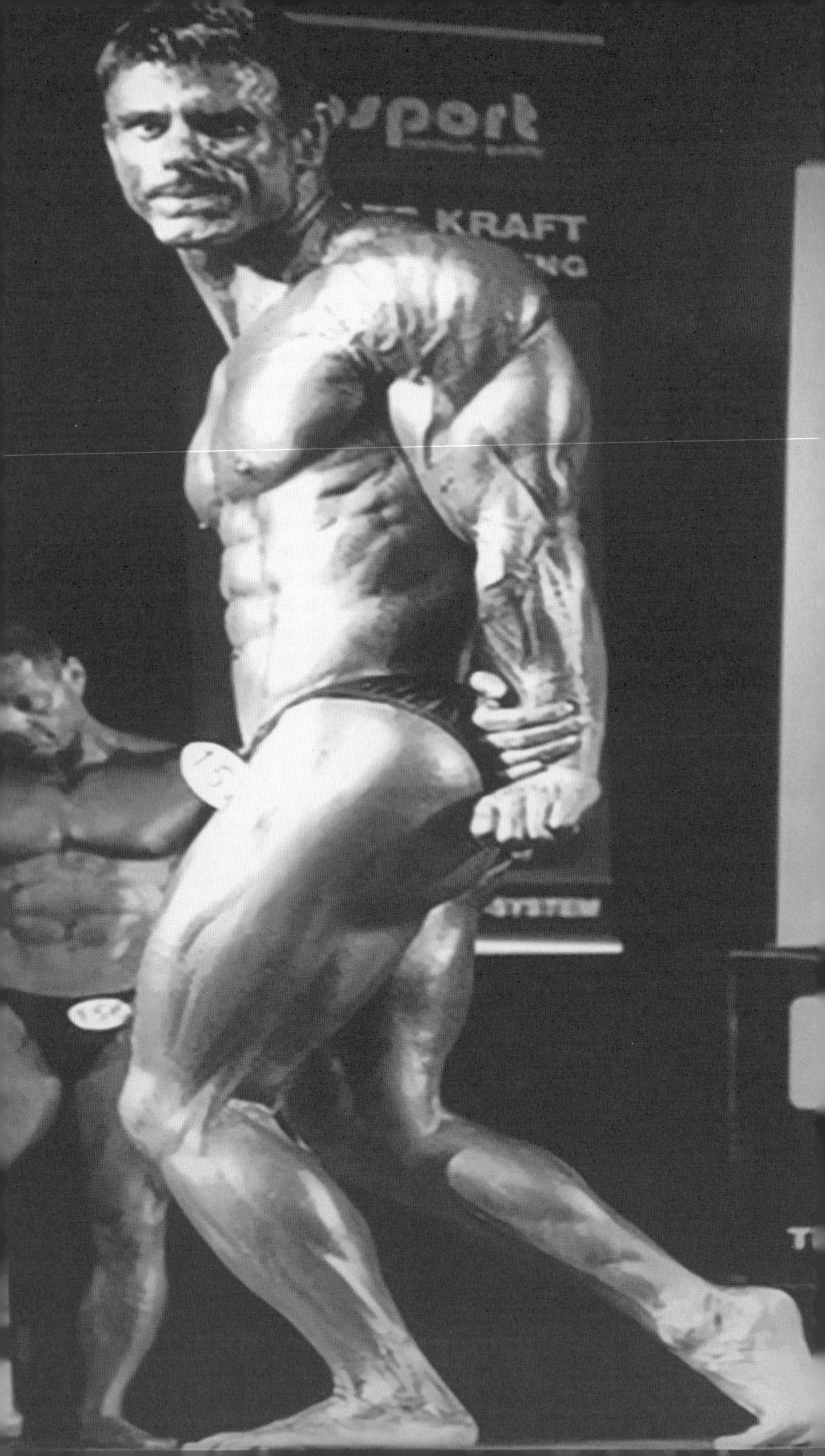
sport
KRAFT

CHAPTER 34

The dream

Mr Universe 2010, round 2, we were now at the venue, waiting for the show to get underway. When the time came we would all go backstage together. One of the lads who was competing had come with his wife, who was luckily willing to help with everyone's tan as well as keeping an eye on the time. This was a big help as timing would be everything, on this occasion more so than ever. The backstage area was scruffy; it was a long hallway with poor lighting that kept flickering on and off. We all had our own one-man cubicles, none of which had any doors, so we had to rely on the light from the aisles, the whole place was dark, quite gloomy. The whole aisle was decorated with a very dated looking brown tile, but at least every cubicle had its own mirror, which for me was always the biggest deal.

So here I was, in my cubicle, fully set with tan already applied, as well as the water and salts at the ready for when the time came. I got the heads up around 25-30 minutes before having to go on stage, and started putting down the salty water, waiting for the magic to happen. It was around 10 minutes before the warming sensation started, followed by the slow yet sure rise in the muscle. The lighting in the cubicle was poor, but still I could see the transformation, as the muscle, even without any prompting, had started to fill out, already feeling heavy. My inner thighs were now like stone and looked enormous, with my back thickening out so much it felt like I had a small rucksack attached to it. The veins were thick, very prominent, and I would appear dry, like the skin on a tree.

Twenty or thirty minutes soon went, and then the whole class was called to the side of the stage as it was nearly time to go on.

The immediate backstage area was very clean and well-lit, with a good-sized mirror, so I could weigh up the competition before going on. My ritual salt-loading had worked better than ever, I had even upped it a little to the point where I had felt more pumped. As I gazed in the mirror my physique appeared how I would have expected it to if I had carried on training for another three years. My shoulders carried huge caps, yet my waistline still appeared tiny. As I looked at the other competitors I could once again see that I had the edge, but was still sceptical due to past experiance.

I got on the scales just before going on stage, I weighed just short of 88kg, my heaviest stage weight ever. Win or lose, I was about to present the most perfect version of me possible, this alone being a massive accomplishment as being seen how I wanted to be seen meant just as much to me as winning, if not more.

It was now show time with the whole line-up out on stage, all the competitors going through their poses. I got the first call out but hadn't taken centre stage, already I felt nervous yet excited. Luckily it wouldn't be long till I had two more call outs, this time both centre stage – now I knew I was in the running. As I came off stage I knew I had been compared with the people who I thought would be in the final five, but I was praying that it was my time to finally shine.

Soon I was back in my little cubicle, waiting around for the night show. I felt more at ease with the judges on this day, as there had been more of them, with only one judge for each country, unlike last time. I was still unsure about the outcome, and was just hoping the night show wasn't that close where they would have to judge us all again, as I could see the separation and the dryness of the muscle had now faded. I wouldn't be looking extraordinary, even when pumped, come the final placings.

When the night show came I had managed to get myself looking half decent, better than I had expected. It was all down to the judges now, but luckily when going out for our final viewing, the judging had already been done. We were lined up and ready for the final placings. I couldn't understand much of what the compere was saying, so I was just trying to catch a part of a name that sounded similar to mine. Straight out of the hat I would hear what sounded like McGowan, this being for sixth place. I had my hands on my face, totally distraught, but on bringing them down and looking down the line I realised it wasn't me, as one of the competitors near the end was now receiving his medal. My heart had bounced into my chest with palpations that felt like I was having heart attack as I had to try and listen on for when my name did finally come up.

It felt like a long time, but it was now down to the final two, with me still in there, my teeth stuck in my lip waiting to hear who would be crowned the new Mr Universe. The next name was announced, it didn't sound like mine, and luckily enough, it wasn't. As I saw the number two competitor bow his head I knew I'd done it, my lifelong dream had finally been met. I was World Champion, with it feeling every bit as good as I thought it would.

I could hear voices over the tannoy but didn't know what they were saying, and even as I stood there looking at the blaze of photographers, I didn't react. I just stood there smiling, taking in the moment, seeing the crowd clapping and smiling for someone they didn't know, yet seemingly respected. I would catch a moment in my heart that would never leave, thinking that at this moment in time there was no one I would rather be than me. The stress, the fuck-ups, had all been worth it just for this one moment in time. With the pressure plug now out there was an overflow of serotonin pleasuring my mind and every thought, this was my life's dream met, it was awesome. From 100% hell to 100% happiness, presenting myself the way I wanted to be seen as well as taking the title as I had hoped. I had lived what had become the nightmare, but was now the dream.

After the overall I went back to the cubicle to take a shower, I was in there a while. On coming out I caught a glimpse in the mirror, my body now pale, already flattened out some. The unique physique I had presented only hours earlier had gone from sight, but I had already pulled off the ultimate illusion that had been needed on the day. As I stood and looked I felt a sense of remorse, like I was saying goodbye to someone I had known and been good friends with a long time, knowing this was the last time I would ever compete. I knew the dream I had lived would live on inside my heart, but also knew that life would now be taking a different path. Leaving bodybuilding on a high was what I had always wanted, the final memory being as pure as the dream that started it.

I didn't go out that night with the rest of the team; instead I relaxed, had some coffee whilst sat on the balcony back at the hotel. Inner peace was what I craved, the only party I needed was what was going on inside my heart and mind at this given time. As I sat staring at the sky, I was re-living the moment over and over, trying to keep it as real and as close to my heart as possible. I was glimpsing the future, feeling ultimately blessed, knowing I had a child on the way. There would be no screams of remorse over not quite finishing what I had started, I would only have to concentrate on being a good father for when the time came. By the end of that night I was looking forward to getting home, finally being able to tell everyone the news about having a child on the way, as well as being able to gloat over my victory.

Back home I was soon telling people the good news, and meeting up for coffees and dinners, as I hadn't been in touch with so many people for such a long time. I still hadn't filled everyone in on the baby news so instead of going round telling people one by one I decided to let everyone know via public media. When getting my picture and story printed by the local newspaper I dedicated my Mr Universe victory to my unborn son. It was a last minute decision, but I thought that if my son ever saw the clipping, when he was older, he would know that he was already in my thoughts as I was winning my ultimate victory.

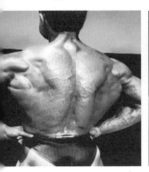

On my return, I went out celebrating with friends, as well as cousin Phil. Late in the evening, when he had had a few beers, Phil kept pointing out that I had achieved what I had wanted, and that now it was time for me to be a dad, to look after my family. He said it that many times, I soon realised he too had been worried whilst I had been training towards the contests, so was now pointing out what my next step in life should be. Phil had been great with me and had helped me through a lot over the past couple of years, I would always be very thankful. I already knew what I had to do – that's why I'd worked so hard.

LIFE WOULD NOW BE TAKING A DIFFERENT PATH

CHAPTER 35

Time to build a new body and mind: my son Michael

Michael John was born on April 6th the following year, and I was there at the birth. On first holding my son I knew life would change. I held my son just seconds after his arrival, and I spoke to him, telling him who I was, that I would always be there for him. My son peered up at me, no tears, no movement, fixated as I spoke, a beautiful honest moment. When I looked up, I saw a room full of teary midwives who had all, unknown to me, been listening throughout the whole of my little speech. Christina, who had been too washed out after the difficult birth to first hold Michael, was looking at me as I stood there holding our little boy. She had a look on her face as if she had been waiting for that moment her whole life. It was a cherished time, my most precious memory. There would be nothing I wouldn't do for my little boy, and I would forever be the doting father. Christina and I would finally get our relationship back on track, becoming a solid unit once more, not just as a couple but as a family.

I would always train, but would never return to the stage, and strangely enough I never wanted to.

I would get back into boxing as well as martial arts, eventually running my own class some years down the line, but once a year I would always put time aside to get myself in good shape, and at no point would I ever stop lifting the weights.

My son Michael was my passion now, seeing him grow up good and have fun would be my main aim.

I stayed good friends with Alex Clarke, we even toured the USA together in 2014. Alex never made it big in bodybuilding, but instead would shift his dedication towards power lifting, in which he thrived, notching up a string of British records, as well as becoming British Champion and silver medallist at the European Games. Damien Lees, the ill-prepared Mr Bury contestant from years earlier, would eventually rise up, battling it out on the world stage and finally winning the Mr Universe in 2015. Damian was one of the few bodybuilders I still followed, knowing where he had started and how far he had come.

Phil Rose, Andy Whittle, Karl Bleakly, Julie Reid, Matt Thomson, Ian Cardoza (Dozer), and (best man) Simon Jaworski were always my go-to guys when wanting advice or someone to talk too, always the best of friends, I would look to these people like my own brothers and sisters.

The old school likes of Big Ste Harrison, Jim Moore, Andy McKenzie, Phil Barber and David Rowlands (Sarge) were all still training. Ste and Phil were actually using walking sticks whilst in the gym, hobbling about between sets. The laughs and the banter went on.

I'm very happy with how life turned out, and I wouldn't change any of it, even the bad times, as I became a better person because of them. I was always thankful about the way I managed to look, and for the titles I'd won, but more thankful about what I had been able to get through, the life lessons learnt. The layers I had built in character would far exceed what I had put on in muscle.

My search for happiness met with a few bumps along the way, but life isn't an exact science, sometimes we have to embrace the madness in order to get to where we need to be, searching for our own truths whilst trying to find who we are, what we stand for.

Would I still be vain, still chasing dreams? Course I would. We are what we are, it doesn't make us bad people, although in some ways it is a kind of disease. The thing is, I like who I am and I'm at my best when most confident, so working hard to keep what I have is still my only real option. I'm acceptant of my age, it brings fresh horizons. I like to look well, feel good, be confident, but now my fitness is more aimed at keeping up with my son, my mind still young in so many ways. Finishing what I start, being true to my word would always be a big deal to me, this book an example of that, another one off the bucket list.

After years of proving my worth, I would finally find inner peace, being able to spot others going down similar paths, being able to help, giving direction and even belief to certain youngsters who've lost their way a little, just like me at their age – I consider this my gift from God.

I hope you've enjoyed my tale, thanks for taking time to read it.

Stay Gold.

God bless.

I was looking at a picture, around 39 years of age, I saw a guy, his name John McLoughlin. He was with a girl, she had blonde hair, blue eyes and was slim in stature, both of them happily smiling, enjoying the bright blue skies, the forefront for the picture being their son Michael who they both deeply loved.

The guy donned a kite-like shape, with large vascular arms and shoulders. He had chiselled, square features carrying a smile that would represent confidence.

I had made it. X

Acknowledgments in regards to this book

Jim Moore. Eamon Kavanagh.

When finishing bodybuilding the thought of writing a book was never far from my mind, but with very limited writing and reading skills I never thought that I'd be able to do it. It wasn't until Eamon (Bury, love and lullabies, the Irish hug) and Jim (a bodybuilder never dies) two characters no more educated than me had written their first books that I realised there were possibilities. When speaking to them both, they told me of ghost writers, spell checks, to write the book how you would say it and not to worry too much about grammar at the early stages. This was step one.

George Lindsey. Jackie Collins.

Throughout 2012 my friend George mentioned to me about writing a book, with the amount of stories I had he said it was something I really needed to do. He said it that many times, I took it as a sign. Soon after, I heard the writer Jackie Collins on TV, talking about getting started writing a book. She said that if it was about a person's life, to start at the earliest memory and to keep going, adding every thought and emotion no matter what the order. She then said that if you only write one page a day, by the end of the year you would have an elaborate book. I was sold, I started my assault the very next day.

John Hartley. Simon Jaworski.

John Hartley, a writer and reviewer who I had worked with and been friends with would do the first ghost write and managed to get the book in some kind of order whilst pointing out the flaws, giving it its first real review. He said the book was fresh, pacey and honest. He said it was if I had woke up one morning, took a gram of whizz, then typed out every thought in my head. He said it needed work but also felt I had a good story and advised me to pursue the book and not to give up on it. Simon, a keen reader, one of my best friends, was the second reviewer of John's version of the book. As much as he tried being positive, his review was honest, and his list of what needed doing, lengthy. With both his and John's reviews quite similar I soon realised there was a lot of work still to do, initially I was not happy. Having to accept the book was far from complete, the re-writes began. Over the next 18 months I re-wrote the book around 40 times, with my love for writing growing more and more. I read Shakespeare for wording purposes as well as other numerous biographies in order to get ideas whilst still trying to make the book my own.

Mark Dagneeno. Tilly Whittle. Karen McLoughlin.

My relationship with the PC has been a turbulent love affair so I'm glad to have had the people above helping with filing, finding the lost, and sending files. I truly am rubbish.

Roger Shelley.

Thanks to Roger for allowing me to use some of his photos throughout the book, also for his time and effort over the years.

Eddie Caldwell. Deborah Turnbil. Gwilym and Jane Hughes.

The final reviews were made by Eddie and Deborah. Eddie said there was a real human story and that he enjoyed it. Deborah said that she found it enlightening. Eddie, the writer of two best sellers (Send In the Clowns, Worn Out Bodies) to do with his professional wrestling career as well as other books in regards to his business (the Northern Institute of Massage) put me on to his publishers, something that had been a closed book up until this point. Jane first reviewed the book, saying that even as a non-bodybuilder, she found it interesting. Working with Gwilym and Jane putting the final pieces together has been great. Very welcoming, and very good at what they do. It's been a real pleasure working with them both.

To all the above, and to everyone who has allowed me to include them in this book or has added help in any way, I thank you all, the story is only here because of you.

Acknowledgments

Family and close friends. Growing up, and in recent years.

To my Mum and Dad. Thank you for all the things I never said thank you for. My shed, the bikes, the skateboards, for the way I was able to live my early life. Sorry about the parties, hahaha. Love you both. X. For my sisters Karen and Debra X. For my auntie Cinnie for looking after me, letting me rent Rocky III and First Blood a thousand times when stopping at yours at the weekends, and thanks for all the support and time you have given me in years gone by X, also to cousins Phil and Andrew. To my cousins, Tina, for the laughs and giving me the honour of being your son Harrison's godfather, and to Uncle Pat X. To Barbara, Elaine and Donna, Auntie Doreen and Uncle Teddy, thanks for looking after me. To cousin Lee, the breaking days. To the Harrisons, my unofficial family while growing up. To Patrick father and son, to Anita, to Paul and mostly to Nick, may God rest his soul, a great influence on me in my early years, and fond memories in regards to the whole family. To Rob Worthington, to Ian Cardoza. To people I've grown closer with over the past couple of years. To Alex and Phil Vyas and to Jet, Janet and Mathew. To Jason Horrocks and to his lovely family. To Andy Whittle, Donna, Tilly, Nick, Chris and Josh, my second family. Same with the Jaworskies. To Simon, Beth, Dave, Carrol, Phil, Neil, Melony and Rob. To my wife Christina and my son Michael, I love you both. XXXXX. Finally to God for the path you have shown me and for the mind and self-belief you've instilled XXXXX. Thank you all. X